GORDON COSBY

HANDBOOK FOR MISSION GROUPS

HANDBOOK FOR MISSION GROUPS

Printed in the United States of America
Library of Congress catalog card number: 73–91551

Scripture quotations marked KJV are from the King James or
Authorized Version of the Bible. Those marked RSV are from the
Revised Standard Version of the Bible, copyrighted 1946 (renewed
1973), 1956 and © 1971 by the Division of Christian Education of
the National Council of the Churches of Christ in the U.S.A., and
are used by permission. Those marked NEB are from The New
English Bible, © The Delegates of the Oxford University Press
and The Syndics of The Cambridge University Press, 1961, 1970,
and are used by permission. Those marked TEV are from Today's
English Version of the New Testament, copyright © American Bible
Society 1966. Those marked Phillips are from J. B. Phillips, The
New Testament in Modern English, © 1958 by J. B. Phillips, pub-
lished by The Macmillan Company. Scripture quotations not marked
are free or personal renderings.

HANDBOOK
FOR
MISSION
GROUPS

If you would like to order additional copies of this book, or other books about the Church of the Saviour, there is an order form in the back of this book for your convenience.

Contents

INTRODUCTION

HISTORY OF
THE CHURCH OF
THE SAVIOUR

History of
The Church of The Saviour
by Elizabeth O'Connor

ROOTS OF A CALL

In this volume are gathered together the concepts and principles of ministry evolved by Gordon Cosby over more than forty years. As a teenager he stood on the street corners of Lynchburg, Virginia, passing out the Gospel of St. John and asking permission to speak with passersby about Jesus Christ, while all the time there grew in him doubts that this was the best way to share his excitement about the faith.

A childhood mentor, Graham Gilmer, filled his imagination with stories of the second coming. When Reverend Gilmer met him on the street he would point one finger upward, lean toward Gordon and say, "Maybe today . . . " He would conclude their conversations with "See you next week, Gordon . . . unless the Lord should come before we meet." This expectation was a part of the Southern church which nurtured its people in doctrine, Scripture, and hymnody. Six weeks of every summer Gordon went to an intensive Bible school where he was given reams of Scripture to memorize, and a gold star when he succeeded in memorizing more than anyone else in the group. Even today from time to time he takes up again this memory work, choosing a chapter from Ephesians, or a passage from the current study of the groups.

9

More often he is memorizing a Psalm. He feels that this is a
way to care for his own life and keep it steeped in the deepest
mysteries of the faith.

All through his childhood he went on Sunday mornings
to the Rivermont Avenue Baptist Church with his father,
who was a confirmed Baptist and a deacon in the church.
In the evening he went with his mother to the Presbyterian
Church where Mr. Gilmer was the pastor. He moved
easily back and forth between these two congregations, absorbing with extraordinary equanimity the more fundamental,
dispensational approach of his mother's church and the more
liberal, patient and inclusive strain of his father's. When
Ernest Campbell became the minister of the Baptist church
and moved into the manse with his wife and three children,
Gordon found in the midst of this family a special home for
his heart and mind. Dr. Campbell put the fifteen-year-old in
charge of the young "Royal Ambassadors," while Mother
Campbell favored his dramatic productions and other imaginative pursuits. His own home had always encouraged his
adventuring and now, when the teenage years imposed on him
the crucial task of establishing a new relationship with his
parents and world, he found himself moving in the warmth
and support of the family in the manse. Often a companion
and always his admirer was nine-year-old Mary, the youngest
daughter in the Campbell family.

When Gordon was still fifteen he and an older brother
stumbled on a one-room church in the foothills of the Blue
Ridge Mountains, about four miles from their home. When
they discovered that it belonged to a black congregation that
had no minister, they offered their services, and were invited
to preach the next Sunday. Gordon gave the sermon that first
Sunday. When the service was over they were both asked to
return. They preached in that church every Sunday for the
next two years, during which time the membership swelled
to forty. They were followed in their pastorate by two younger

brothers. A first congregation must surely have a larger responsibility than is usually acknowledged for the response to and care of a young minister. This little mountain church encouraged the gifts of their youthful pastors. They punctuated Gordon's sermons with their amens and in one way or another let him know that they were hearing what he said. One old man who sat at the end of the second row, on the right, interrupted each sermon at least once to shout, "Say it again, Brother. Say it again." In the young preacher grew up a confidence that was never to leave him. It was confidence in the power of the Word, and in himself as a proclaimer of that Word.

After high school he went to work in his father's savings and loan company to be groomed for a place in the business. All of his free time was spent in the activities of the church or at the manse. Around the Campbell's kitchen table or in the living room where young friends gathered, the talk more often than not turned to the church. These were the hours that excited Gordon and helped him to decide that his father's business was not for him—that he was to be a minister. Something broke within him, so that later he was to describe *call* as "a sense of being dealt with by that which is ultimate, of knowing that one was born to this, that one has found one's place in the scheme of things—in salvation history."

Then he simply announced to his family that he was going to seminary. "I did not go the usual route," he says. "If I had written ahead I don't think that they would have accepted me. I didn't have any credentials." Two years after he began his seminary training at Southern Baptist Theological Seminary in Louisville, he began his college work at Hampden-Sydney College, not far from Lynchburg. He never was able to put his roots down very deeply in either the seminary or the academic community. During this period he had become the minister of a church in a nearby railroad town, and being the minister to these people was always more absorbing to

him. These were also the years that he courted Mary Campbell who had grown up at last and was enrolled in Randolph-
Macon College. Despite these diverse activities, in 1942, four
and one-half years later, he was graduated magna cum laude
from the college and in the same year completed his seminary
training and was ordained to the ministry.

This was also the year that he and Mary were married.
Mary was beautiful and gracious with a passion for the church
that was like his own. She complemented his shy seriousness,
and was to add to every church occasion the festive note,
which was in part her reaction to paper plate suppers in
church basements. One man said of the Potter's House whose
decor she had helped select, "It's the only place I know where
the atmosphere takes care of you." This is true of all the
rooms where she has been. Flowers stand poised in a special
way, candles are always lighted and the music playing. One
feels *received* by the room itself.

War Distills a Mission

Gordon was serving a congregation outside of Washington,
D.C., when he enlisted in the army and was sent overseas as
chaplain of the 327th Glider Infantry Regiment, 101st Airborne Division. In the winter of 1944 in England and later,
on the broken terrain of Belgium, he began to work with concepts of ministry that were to be built upon, deepened, and
refined over all the years to come. Like every other regimental
chaplain he found himself responsible for the spiritual life of
more than three thousand men who would be scattered over
great distances and almost always under the threat of immediate death. In many other settings he was to reform and
restate the questions he began to ask then: How does one
build the church in these circumstances? How can one be the
church?

Reflecting on those war years Gordon now sees that his
situation then was not very different from that of the minister

of any congregation made up of men and women who throughout the week are spread out over large geographical areas in widely divergent places of work, many of which are oppressive structures that rob them of their lives without their knowing. How can one man, or even a team ministry, be pastor and prophet to the members of a congregation with whom they have very little possibility of developing any kind of depth relationship for any length of time?

Perhaps, in a way that might otherwise not have happened, the battlefields of Holland and Belgium drew into sharp focus for Gordon the questions with which every minister in some way struggles, if he takes with any seriousness the building of the church of Christ. Knowing as he did that he could not minister in depth to even two hundred men in a stationary situation, Gordon was painfully aware of how impossible it would be to meet the desperate needs of thirteen companies in combat. He moved quickly and decisively to bring into being a little church in each of the companies.

First he identified the man in each company who seemed most spiritually mature and, in effect, ordained him to the ministry as the "sky pilot" for his company, a process that we of The Church of The Saviour now refer to as "the calling forth of gifts." He then began a miniature seminary to train these men for the ministry and to help them identify and name an assistant. Around these pairs of men formed small bands who became responsible for the spiritual life of the others in their companies.

These little churches within the companies became known as the Airborne Christian Church, for their congregations were the men who were to be dropped by glider on the world's battlefields. They were also the forerunners of the early Church of The Saviour fellowship groups which later evolved into mission groups. As often as war allowed, Gordon met with the newly ordained clergy in a training program that included the sharing of their ministries. Here also was the beginning of the design for our own School of Christian Living, which is very much a seminary for the training of the laity. Before the Airborne Church left the English countryside, it had outgrown its borrowed chapel and moved into a school gymnasium.

Other war experiences began to shape his ministry. There was the night that seven men were selected from his company to infiltrate the enemy lines, make observations, and feel out enemy strength. They were to leave one hour before midnight, stay until almost daybreak, and return if possible. In all likelihood only three, or two, or one would make it back, but such a mission would provide valuable information for the activities of the whole regiment the following day. In the "terribly long and terribly short" hours before eleven, most of the men came to talk with their young chaplain. They brought pictures of the babies that they had never seen and of their wives and mothers. They left with him trinkets and valuables to send home "in case," and always they put into his hands the address of someone. They left scribbled notes. One man came to make his commitment to Jesus. He had put it off long enough. When eleven o'clock came they slipped off into the darkness.

Through the night Gordon waited and prayed and thought about all that might be taking place. As he listened to the sporadic barking of machine gun fire in the distance, he pondered the pictures of their families at home and hoped that God would comfort them when they got the news. He wondered if one or two would get back, and which ones they would be. And what of those who would die? Would the words that he had said to them have any meaning? Would the men be hindered or helped by those words when they stood in the presence of God?

That night he saw in those seven men Everyman and Everywoman. To none of us is given to know the time or the day, but the fact is . . . "Maybe today." What does it

mean for the church to be God's waiting people? Can our
waiting be meaningful to others, if we are not obedient while
we wait? What does it mean to be "radically obedient?"—
"radically committed?" What must our life style be?

It was almost dawn when a lone figure came through the
morning mist. Gordon thanked God. And then came another,
and yet another—until all seven were back. Such a reunion he
had never seen. Their words tumbled over each other, "This is
what happened to me." "Remember the first heavy exchange
. . . ?" "How did you get by that sentry?" "This is the way it
was . . ." Seven dead men were alive—together again. There
were new possibilities—things could be and happen once
more.

That night became for him a parable of the church when
she authentically gathers—"A group of people who have
known that they were bound over to the power of death,
stumble on a treasure and that treasure is Christ, miracle of
miracles, doors that were closed open, gates of bronze are
broken down. The words spill out as they try to tell one
another what happened, and how it happened, and of a
Presence that was there."

All through the war the storytelling went on—more often
when the men broke open C-rations and sat around eating
and talking. Under the circumstances the usual defenses were
gone, and quickly their conversations moved to a deeper
sharing of themselves. When men are involved intensively in
a common danger, and do not know whether they will be
around the next night, let alone the next week, they move
with directness to satisfy the basic human need to be heard
and to be known. Even gruff and untutored men listened
without judgment and treated with tenderness each other's
stories. Deep bonds of friendship were forged.

"We were drawing easily," said Gordon, "on the tremendous capacity for intimacy that is in each of us. I think this is
why men sometimes romanticize war. We had that sense of

community that we all yearn for and which many of these
men had never known before and would never know again."
It is not strange that Gordon Cosby has become the minister
of a church whose unwritten covenant is that we will be
enablers of each other in the telling of our stories.

In retrospect one finds other wartime experiences shaping
Gordon's ministry. As he shared his understanding of Scripture with men from different expressions of the church and
they shared with him out of varied experiences, their excitement about the faith grew, and they knew once more an unexpected communion with one another. In those incredible
moments when bread was broken and Christ stood in their
midst, Gordon committed himself to being the minister of
an unknown church that would be ecumenical in its spirit, in
dialogue with all the churches—indeed, with all men. He began to write home to Mary about the church that would later
write into its member's commitment the words, "I will seek
to be Christian in all relations with my fellowmen, with other
nations, groups, classes and races."

There was another who shared his dream of the church.
While his regiment was still in England, he had become
friends with Carl Werner, a large, vital and exuberant man,
who was excited about what a community might be that took
Christianity seriously. In their youthful enthusiasm it seemed
to them both that such a church would surely be empowered
by the Spirit and infuse with its life the whole of Christendom. There would be an end to war. Men would enter into
the peace of Christ, and put aside their arms—not because it
was good strategy, or something laid on their consciences to
do, but because there would be no need for weapons anymore.

Werner wrote home to the girl to whom he was engaged,
describing the church and suggesting that when the war was
over they go to Washington and help to get it started. She
not only wrote back yes, but said that she had a friend who
was a potential donor. "Please send a prospectus." They began work on it immediately and had the last draft almost com-

pleted when the invasion of Normandy began. After landings were made, the intense fighting gave them little time, but they still managed to meet and plan the church. On the 16th of June, 1944, after days of fighting so fierce that they did not even try to see each other, Gordon picked up the casualty list and Carl Werner's name leapt out from all the others.

He spent that long and anguished day picking up the bodies of men and loading them onto trucks and then unloading them in a designated field. There were literally hundreds of bodies piled in that field when he left with the alcoholic jeep driver for a lonely field several miles away where he was to bury the dearest friend he had—the man who had befriended with him a vision only dimly seen. In the spiritual biography that he wrote later for his own small group he told something of that day:

Powerfully disciplined German Panzer troops were a few miles away, covering the Normandy countryside. With a damp New Testament in my hand opened at 1 Corinthians 15, save for one wizened alcoholic at my side, I was alone with an impossible dream. I knew the power of envy, a strange envy. The envy of my friend who was experiencing that which was denied to me for awhile. I knew the power of the resurrection in the midst of the unbearable loneliness and death. From that moment I knew that I could go on alone, if necessary. Faithfulness to what I had seen did not depend upon human support. Those agonizing years were to make me singularly unconcerned with "success." Also I felt delivered in large measure from the fear of death. I was to be close to it many times during the next months, but its sting had been removed. The impact of this quality of experiencing is difficult to describe. It is so vivid and real afterwards it is as hard to disbelieve as before it was hard to believe. There is another realm! To touch it is to live. To become immersed in it is the only worthwhile pursuit, to give it to others, the deepest joy.

As the war went on and the 101st Airborne Division moved into Germany, Gordon's uneasiness about the church grew.

Always he had felt the discrepancy between what the church proclaimed and what she embodied in her structure and life style. Now he was observing day by day men who had been raised in all the structures of the church, and yet were no more men of faith than those raised outside her life. Under the pressures of fatigue and suffering, removed from law, order, family—the externals that in normal times keep things together for us all—they were confused and unable to detach themselves from the mores of a culture that sanctioned a different morality for war than for peace. It was a lawless morality that was to prevail for months in occupied Germany as though the peace had not been made. Again he was pondering the question of integrity of membership in the Body of Christ. What were the structures of the church that would so nurture men and women in discipleship that Christ would always have first priority in their lives no matter what the circumstances?

For two and a half years he and Mary had written back and forth to each other their dreams for the unnamed church, continuing by mail the conversation begun so long before around a kitchen table. Somewhere in their writing they began to feel that it would be much easier to fulfill their dream outside the denominational framework. For one thing, their church would have to be interracial, and for another, it would have to be free to experiment with new structures. The churches of the 1940s allowed for neither.

BUILDING A COMMUNITY

Fired by the vision of speaking a wondrous gospel through all the lands, Gordon came home to begin The Church of The Saviour. He and Mary, together with Elizabeth-Anne, Mary's sister, who was in training at Garfield Hospital in Washington, D.C., began holding an evening vesper service for the nurses—one of their first efforts to let others know that they were "a church."

The School of Christian Living opened with one student, a

slow, conservative and unlettered lad whom they had known in Madison Heights, Virginia. Billy had no idea of what he was getting into when he moved into the Washington area and looked up his old friends. Ernest Campbell, at that time the minister of a church in Alexandria, made the living room of his house available as a classroom. For six months Gordon met with Billy to teach him doctrine, Christian growth, and Bible; meantime they struggled to determine what gift he might exercise on behalf of the new church. At long last they enthusiastically decided that it was running the mimeograph machine. Thereafter Gordon taught him as they worked together on mimeographing. When the year was over Billy was transferred by his employer to Iowa, leaving Gordon to wonder whether that first lone recruit might not have effected his own transfer in order to be free of involvement in an enterprise that was always slightly bewildering. In any case, Billy's departure did not lessen the ardor of his instructor, who remained firmly convinced that the school, or "little seminary," was essential training ground if the church was to have an inward life and move with any force in the world.

That year with Billy was in its way typical of Gordon Cosby's ministry. He had issued a call to church and the Lord had sent one person; so he treated that uncomplicated youth as though the whole future of the church depended on him. In time he was to believe even more deeply in ordinary persons, who in turn were to believe more deeply in themselves. This is probably why the community that has come into being under his leadership gives so little attention to credentials—a fact which is at first disappointing to those who come presenting degrees and programs to help us out of the trouble we are forever in. In the more than twenty years that I have been in this community no one has ever asked me which college I attended, although ministers from other places inquire about this as well as about my theological training. I have to tell them that I did not make it very often to grade school, but that I put in four hard years in high school. When they indicate that this is very fine, I am never sure whether they are trying to communicate acceptance of me, or whether their attitude implies a widespread conviction that our educational institutions are failing to provide the training needed to conduct our affairs and build community—always a work of art. If we are to build the church we must each day learn things we were never taught.

Paradoxically, this community which takes so little notice of degrees gives inordinate attention to education. Five classes are still required for membership in the church: Old Testament, New Testament, Doctrine, Christian Growth, and Ethics. In addition, in every eleven-week semester a half-dozen other classes dealing with some aspect of the inward-outward journey are offered. They vary in content and focus, and range all the way from "discovery of self" to journal writing and contemplation. Classes are taught by those whose gifts identify them as teachers. They are always persons well informed in a subject they have pursued because of an absorbing interest. We have discovered that people usually communicate well the subjects that have caught something deep within themselves. The usual student-teacher relationship seldom prevails. Most of the classes are conducted in the manner of a seminar with each student presenting findings from the application of the week's assignment in the living out of his or her life.

Completion of two eleven-week classes in the school is a requirement for internship in one of the small groups. The fact that the five classes required for full membership take approximately two years, always gives rise to the question, "How do you manage to find people who will go to school for that long a time?" The answer is that we do not try. Most of the 150 people who move through the school each year do not stop to consider that the classes are required for membership. They are not there to meet standards, but because it is a stimulating place to be. Most of us who have been in the membership for any length of time return to the school now and then for a new course that is being offered, or to review in our more "informed state" an old class.

When a person has had the equivalent of the subject matter covered in any one of the required courses, and if his small group concurs, we will waive the requirement for that class. The request, however, is seldom made. In the beginning we rather automatically gave special dispensation to ministers who came to be with us. After all, we reasoned, a man who has been to seminary and preached in a church would not need classes in New and Old Testament. We changed our attitude, however, when these same men later complained that they felt robbed—as though they had missed out on something intangible but essential for their belonging to the whole.

In the early days theology was taught and learned while the work of introducing prospective members to the community went on. The school assumed a more formal structure only as the church grew. One of the most powerful supporters was Mother Anne Campbell who was teaching a Bible class at her husband's large, conventional Baptist church. She talked so enthusiastically about the church that was getting underway that, with her encouragement, several good Baptists ventured over into the new fold, and then they, in turn, lured a few more. Elizabeth-Anne was also issuing frequent calls at Garfield Hospital, while Gordon shared his life and dream with every likely and unlikely soul that crossed his path. The street evangelist of Lynchburg now had as his mission field the un-churched of the nation's capital. Even so, at the end of the year the whole congregation numbered only nine.

STRUGGLE FOR INTEGRITY

These nine were bound together by a covenant written by Gordon's brother, Peter Cosby, and printed on a small blue card that each member was to sign and carry. Included were such high and lofty statements as, "I unreservedly and with abandon commit my life and destiny to Jesus Christ, promising to give him a practical priority in all the affairs of life " Through the years only a rare person ever questioned his or her capacity to fulfill that covenant. On the back of the card, however, were printed the disciplines that translated into specific and concrete terms the community's understanding of what that covenant meant. Over these more prosaic, more explicit statements there was to be a falling away of would-be members, who felt some of the sayings to be too hard. The founding members, often petitioned to change them, could never bring themselves to do it. They had hammered out those disciplines in order to become the kind of community they envisioned. The disciplines also embodied their understanding of the nature of the church. They had included a discipline of praying because they understood the church of Jesus Christ to be a praying people. They had covenanted to meditate on Scripture every day because the church is a people informed and instructed by the word of God. They had agreed to give proportionately beginning at ten percent of their gross income because this was essential if they were to have a thrust into the world that would be exciting to them as well as to others. It early became evident that to reduce any one discipline was to reduce them all, for each individual struggled at a different point. One person who had difficulty with a set time of prayer would find the tithing concept quite acceptable, while another found the prayer discipline easy but the parting with his money an unspeakable hardship.

The small fellowship was very early confronted with temptation from within their own company. Their incomes were all meager. Elizabeth-Anne made $20 a month. Frank Cresswell was an intern doctor holding his young family together on $120 a month. Gordon was working part time for a small Baptist church so that he would be free to spend the rest of his time with the new church. All were hampered financially

—except for one member who, substantially employed, lent an air of financial respectability. It was he who questioned the concept of "corporate disciplines" and "corporate responsibility." It was then that the little group began to be aware of the costliness of its call. They had to examine at a new level their definition of church as a voluntary community with a clearly defined life style. They talked for hours and hours, confronted and questioned their own motivations and convictions, and named aloud their fear of destroying the delicate fabric of the fellowship in the name of building it. There was no shortcut through the painful work of coming face to face with the knowledge that treasured friends whose call and commitment led them by a different path would have to be allowed to leave.

Perhaps the experience of those weeks instructed the little community to write into its constitution the principle of annual recommitment. They agreed that during the third week of each October, having reflected on the commitment they had previously made, they would, if they could, again sign the membership book. Then, on Sunday they would stand and say together the covenant beginning, "I come today to renew my commitment to this local expression of the church. . . ."

October came to be known as the month of "recommitment blues," a term that gives some hint of the work going on in our lives. Gordon Cosby was to say that this concept, perhaps more than any other, was the one destined to be the most helpful in retaining integrity of membership. It was, and still is, a time for raising into fuller consciousness the high call of God in Christ, and our commitment to live out that call in one particular segment of his church. We had structured into our lives a period of self-examination against the backdrop of the covenant we had made and the disciplines we had pledged ourselves to keep. Sometimes, when October came we were made aware that we had become lukewarm, were in the process of drifting away, and were in need of help.

Occasionally a person discovered that she or he really "wanted out" but was fearful of abandoning the community or of being abandoned by the community. However, moving out of membership at recommitment time rarely meant moving out of the church. Often a person has taken this step and then rejoined after an interval that can be very long or very short. Rather than a sign of defection, withdrawal from the membership is often a sign of health—a time when a person takes the distance needed for seeing again that choices exist for renewing old decisions or making new ones. At the same time, the principle of annual recommitment offers recurring assurance that the members, in freedom, have bound themselves together under a covenant that not only describes who they are but also will help them in their journeying to where they want to be.

The community's first quarters was an old rooming house complete with housekeeper and several roomers who stayed on and were caught up in the contagious exuberance of the new occupants. The previous residents helped with the painting—and cast their lot with the odd but captivating band of newcomers. The question then was: would there be money enough to buy the paint to carry on the next day's work? That question is again a part of the scene, for paint is now needed for two apartment houses in the inner city. We know now that the community being born then was always to smell slightly of turpentine and have paint on its shoes. For more reasons than one its latest mission bears the appropriate name of Jubilee Housing.

In those days we were blissfully ignorant of the houses for which we were to be the agents of transformation. Only a few years went by before the first quarters were obviously inadequate, and we acquired a twenty-three-room house and began again to scrub, scrape and paint. This old Victorian mansion still remains the headquarters and place of worship for the whole community. The corporate indebtedness was huge. We were then about thirty-two persons, probably twenty of whom were employed, and we owed about one hundred thousand dollars. Our distinction at that time was that we probably had the highest per capita indebtedness of any church in the country.

The work of renovation on the new building was scarcely completed when the group further increased its indebtedness by the purchase of 176 acres of land in the country. The membership had grown to thirty-six, and there were another fifty or sixty persons taking classes. Again there was a farmhouse to restore and a lodge to build. After that the restoration efforts of the group were to be employed at its place of mission.

STRUGGLE FOR MISSION

The mission of the community now became the primary issue. The gifts of teaching had been identified, the school was offering the basic classes every semester, and the members met in small fellowship groups. The groups were committed to worship, prayer, study, and corporate outreach. Not one of them, however, was ever able to agree on what its outreach would be. We sat in our little groups and discussed it week after week, but all our prayer, imagining, and investigation produced nothing which caught the common soul. We were slow to recognize that the very diversity of gifts made it impossible to find a corporate mission. One person would say, "Let's have a street music group." The next person would reply, "I'm tone deaf." Someone would suggest working with alcoholics, and another would answer, "Not for me." The exploration went on and on, and it seemed there was always someone to put out the fire in another.

Somewhere in the midst of it all it became clear that there was only one way to solve our dilemma. If the church was to find servant structures, the small groups had to be formed around focused and defined missions with each mission also committed to an inward journey of prayer, worship and study. This concept seems very simple to us now, but in those early days there were no models and no guidelines, nor was there any confirmation of that toward which we struggled. Just about that time we came across what seemed like a very promising book. The writer was describing the very things we were committed to; more than that, he promised to offer help before he was done. Chapter followed chapter with no yielding of secrets. The pages were running out when the writer suggested that those wanting to pursue the matter further turn to the appendix. There one was advised to write to The Church of The Saviour in Washington, D.C.!

Gordon Cosby still feels that the churches, in their quest for structures that nurture life in people, must know that they are venturing into new territory, and that the resources for their exploration rest in the tremendous untapped potential of their own people. The difficulty is that we so often lack confidence in ourselves and in our companions and search for the answers in some other place.

The decision to abandon the small fellowship groups in order to form mission groups was again a tearing one. For one thing it meant parting with those with whom we had shared the very depths of ourselves, and with whom we had deep bonds. Secondly, some of us were not at all convinced it was essential, and thirdly, there was really no place for us to go. When it came right down to it, we had never taken seriously our own responsibility to hear call and to issue it. At one point it seemed that we were all milling around in a kind of anguished confusion, as though we, too, had been brought out of Egypt to die in the wilderness.

In the midst of the confusion Gordon walked with the sureness of one headed for a far better place. He stopped to reason, comfort and confront, but there was no question of the direction in which he was set. Furthermore, it seemed not to disturb him that some felt torn up and anxious. To him it

was a highly creative time—all a part of breaking up camp and
moving toward the Lord who waited outside the camp. "To be
a disciple," he explained, "is to share in the life of which the
Cross is the culmination. In the evolution of an individual,
there is an inner work to be done, and that is always costly."
In his preaching and in his conversation he was reminding his
own little band that the call of God was a call to create a new
kind of community that would be distinguished by its human-
ness. It would be so human that those in it would do whatever was needed so that every one in the world might be free.
He was reissuing the call to which we had first made response.
Later he was to tell the moderators of the small mission
groups, "There comes a time in the life of every group when
it loses sight of its goals and must choose them again. It will
be your job to sound again the call, to be the bearer of the
vision—articulating it in your own life and helping others to
see it."

WAITING FOR CALL

To help us through our impasse we formed classes in
Christian Vocation. In these classes we were taking a deeper
and longer look at the whole matter of Call as having to do
with the transcendent—the being grasped by that which is
greater than we. We began with the basic assumption of the
New Testament that there was no way to be the church except by the call of Christ, and that there were a number of
dimensions to this call:

First, it was a call to a relationship with the Father as
intimate as the one which Christ knew.

Second, it was a call to being persons in community with
others responding to the same call, surrendering something
of our own authority that we might have a shared life and
bring into existence a new community where the nature of
the relationships would be such that each person would be
called fully into being.

Third, it was a call to an inward development—a call to

change. We were to overcome those obstacles in ourselves which held us back and kept us from growing up into the full stature of Christ. The call of Christ was a call to die to the old self in order to become the new creation.

Fourth, and not last, it was a call to move out—to discover where we were to lay down our lives—to take up the stance of the suffering servant, and make witness to the power of Jesus Christ at work in us.

The class dealt primarily with the fourth dimension. If the church is a *sent* people, where was Christ sending each of us? To what segment of the world's need were we to make response? We began each session by sitting for an hour in the silence, feeling that if any word was being addressed to us we had more opportunity of hearing it in the stillness of our own souls. Part of the work of the hour was to center deeply enough in ourselves to be in touch with our most central wish. Somehow we had then, and have now, the conviction that our wishes lie very close to "who we are" and what we are to be doing, and that to be in communion with them is to have a sense of being dealt with by the One who is Other.

We discovered in this class that too many of us had moved into our vocations without any sense of being called to them. "Vocation," Gordon said, "has the element of knowing that if you respond to the call, you are faithful to your own inner being and you are enhanced by it. Your own awareness converges with some need out yonder and intersects with it in such a way that you have the sense that you were born to this." Jesus said, "I must be about my Father's business."* He knew. It is an inner knowing.

When the time of silence was over we timidly put forward any intimations of direction that had come to us. We were so uncertain and so consumed by misgiving that the question was inevitable: "Is not one's call often shot through with self-doubt?"

---

* Luke 2:49, KJV.

We decided that doubt is a dimension that oftentimes is there, and that there is a time to move on in spite of it. In fact, we agreed that if anyone were too dogmatic about call, he or she needed to question it because there is always the possibility of acting out of some compulsive need rather than genuine call. Frequently along with the call comes the feeling that one is not up to it. There is a sense of unworthiness in relationship to what one sees. "Who am I to be called to bring into existence anything so significant? Surely there are other people more qualified to do it." This is what Moses felt. He was forever protesting that Yahweh could choose someone better equipped for the job, someone who talked more convincingly than he did. Jeremiah said flatly that he was too young, even going to the extreme in that declaration, " 'I am only a child.' But the Lord said, 'Do not call yourself a child; for you shall go to whatever people I send you and say whatever I tell you to say.' "*

All of us resist in some way the new thing into which we are drawn that demands a whole new dimension of creativity on our part. We do not want to be responsible in this way. "It may be," says Gordon, "that if a person responds too eagerly, he is not seeing the whole picture and is not aware of the problems of implementation, so that he goes into it with large areas of unconsciousness."

Despite our expectancy and all the assurance and encouragement we gave to each other, no one was "addressed by a Voice," which is the real meaning of "having a vocation."‡ Perhaps it was because we were too disbelieving, or too unpracticed in the process in which we were engaged, or perhaps it was that we were too literal in our understanding of call— expecting somehow that God was going to descend out of heaven and summon us as we sat with heads bowed. Actually

* Exod. 3–4; Jer. 1:6–7, NEB.
‡ For a fuller discussion of these terms, see Carl G. Jung, *The Development of Personality*, Collected Works of C. G. Jung, vol. 17 (Princeton, N.J.: University Press, 1954), pp. 167–86.

call was to come to most of us through the ordinary events of
life, which were to be extraordinary events because we brought
to them a new quality of asking and listening.

In the spring of that long year Gordon and Mary made what
might have been a routine trip to a church in New England
where Gordon gave the Lenten address. They found the
atmosphere in the church cold and the congregation unbend-
ing, and they left with a feeling of wanting to put that whole,
dark church far behind them. They drove for a long distance,
before they stopped at a country inn and were given the last
available room, which happened to be above the tavern. The
noises from that tavern drifted up to them and disturbed their
sleeping, but somewhere in the night Gordon thought,
"Christ would be more at home in that tavern than back in
the church we just left."

The next morning he and Mary had breakfast in a small
restaurant across the street from the inn, and there again the
friendliness and warmth made him think, "Christ would be
more at home in this restaurant than in the church." He went
home to tell the class in Christian Vocation that a way should
be found to take the church to the restaurants of the city. Out
of the discussion that followed emerged the idea of a coffee
house, and in the naming of it call was heard. Gordon knew
that he was called and several others knew that they were
called. Others felt that it was not for them, but encouraged
the sounding of the call in the larger congregation. Twelve
people responded, and the mission was under way.

When The Potter's House finally opened a year later we
had been joined by others, and with everyone working two
and sometimes three times a week we were able to keep open
on six nights. The disciplines for members and intern members were hammered out and within a few months there were
eight or ten people to staff each of the nights and thus each
night had its own mission group. Here we were to develop
and expand the concept of gifts that Gordon covers in the

chapter entitled "The Calling Forth of the Gifts." People who had not been able to understand what a coffee house had to do with church caught the idea the moment they went through the doors. The Potter's House, on that ghetto street, remains a sign of hope—"its own excuse for being."

In the meantime others began to hear call and to issue call, and new missions were born. Three were committed to keeping strong the home base and equipping us for ministry. The first of these was the Retreat Mission Group, which had among its responsibilities the nurturing of the mission groups in the whole concept of retreat, so that finally a Retreat Center was established that enabled each group to make a retreat once a year. Then there was the group that had as its concern the children of the church—a commitment which was eventually to develop mission groups for children. Another group took on the responsibility of the School of Christian Living, incorporating into that structure the whole concept of mission as it was being developed. Our sermons, classes, and conferences were all concerned with helping others to discover gifts and hear call. We found ourselves so often asking, "What is it that you want to do now that you are six?" "What would you like to do now that you are fifty and the children are away and you have the new gift of time?" "What do you want to do now that you are eighty, and have the resources of a whole lifetime to bring to every work?"

"What would you like to do?" is a question we still ask indiscriminately—of the very young and the very old, of poor and rich, oppressed and oppressors, and then we listen very carefully and take with utmost seriousness what a person says.

As more people began to hear call, more missions came into being. These calls were first explored in the small community of one's close friends, and later in the larger community. We began to know that it can be painful to have one's vision tested by people who are not friendly to it, or who ask what seem to be unimportant questions. We soon discovered, however, that the corporate input forced us to refine and sharpen our thinking and enlarge the dream. In the end we worked out a procedure requiring every mission to be confirmed by the church council. This never meant to us that everyone had to be enthusiastic about every call.

Oftentimes we have to be willing to let another move even when we have large reservations. Our learning to do this with a certain degree of ease is that factor which, probably more than any other, accounts for the proliferation of mission groups in the community of The Church of The Saviour. This does not mean that we easily deal with anxiety, angry feelings and ego needs. Some have learned slowly to reason with unreasonable fears, and for them the pain has been very great. Others have discovered that there is nothing lonelier in all the world than to live in the midst of those who know community and to feel in one's own heart estranged, or to be at the center of a gift-evoking group where there is no one to receive what one has to give, and from time to time some of us find ourselves in those desolate stretches of land. Always, too, we have found it incredibly hard to hold to the concept of the inward and outward journeys. We early discovered that not many persons want both dimensions. Weighted heavily on one side or the other, most of us struggle intensely to keep them in any kind of creative tension in our individual and our corporate lives.

A Mission Is Defined

Every mission group has known not only its beginning excitement and small triumphs but its extremely difficult times. For The Potter's House one such time came in the spring of 1965. Having freely released a number of its people to follow other calls and to join new missions, it found itself understaffed. This made The Potter's House groups especially vulnerable to the arguments of those who wanted to help staff it without subscribing to all the disciplines or participating in the School of Christian Living. We were too often won to thinking that not everyone can travel the same path, and that some people were just too individualistic to subscribe to our recommendations. So we began to make exceptions, which we still do, but the exceptions became the norm, and the whole character of the evenings began to change. Fortunately, it didn't work very well. Group members were inconsistent in their attendance, and when they did come they ceased to find in what was happening that which had attracted them in the first place. Even the customers dropped away, and the receipts went down and put the whole enterprise in the red.

One weekday afternoon The Potter's House Council, made up of one member from each of the groups, met and accepted what was an astounding and risky recommendation. What Gordon in essence proposed was that we agree to close The Potter's House, that all persons then staffing it be released from their commitment, and that on the following Sunday a new call be issued, reforming The Potter's House around highly disciplined groups.

"What if enough people do not respond?" we asked. "At least now we can keep it open, and try to work out something."

"I think that would be a mistake," he replied. "If we do not make the issue sharp enough, it will have no teeth in it."

"But," someone said, "it is going to stir up a lot of feeling and anxiety."

Gordon thought that just might be a good thing. He felt that we had let the whole matter drift into the present state, that although we had issued warnings before, we had not dealt with them.

I can remember that afternoon: his lounging in the chair in a characteristic way and enjoying our surprise, and by his very attitude injecting expectancy and challenge into a meeting that was shrouded in gloom when it started. Before long we were caught up in what he was proposing, though I vividly recall thinking at the time, "We would never have come to this on our own," and wondering what made him so much freer and more trusting than we seemed to be.

The answer may lie in what he said to a friend who asked him a question he is often asked, "What do you think the future of the church is?" He replied, "I have never had a helpful answer to that question. Have no idea. I do not know what the judgments of God are or what will be the breakthroughs of God's power." Then he stopped for a long pause and added, "I do not need the church to have a visible or successful future in order for me to feel safe as a person. I'm glad to leave it to God's sovereignty. It is his church—not mine."

The call that Gordon issued that Sunday morning was to a more rigorous and disciplined inward journey than any of the small groups had corporately adopted. The time that we set aside each day to work on the disciplines was increased from a minimum of thirty minutes to fifty minutes. Three new disciplines were added to those that the membership kept: daily writing in a journal, a report of accountability to be made each week to the group's spiritual director, and a weekly day of fast. The day of fast has become an optional discipline, but most of the small groups now keep a journal on some consistent basis and write a weekly report for the group's spiritual director.

The call sounded by Gordon that Sunday came as good news to many, and The Potter's House entered into a whole new era of creativity. This was the year that the riots had been contained in the surrounding streets only by the threatening presence of a large police force. The groans of the oppressed were heard everywhere, and The Potter's House became the seedbed of new missions. It was now open during the day, and it was also opening every morning to give a hot breakfast to forty neighborhood schoolchildren, pending the time the

local school could expand its program. We bought a small
house in the neighborhood and initiated a program for senior
citizens that included a hot midday meal. Bit by bit we were
being freed from old ways and customs. We had once claimed
Thanksgiving and Christmas days for ourselves and closed the
doors to a lonely city. Somewhere along the way we began
serving Thanksgiving and Christmas dinners for all who would
come. Many of our families gathered up their own children
and arrived bearing armloads of food as well. Poor and rich,
black and white, well and sick, young and old were there, and
there was always enough for all who came. The tradition is
now four years old, and for some it seems the only way to
celebrate these holidays, but another segment of the community gathers around a groaning board at our retreat farm,
and they tell the same story.

The Covenant Is Questioned

Our grappling with the disciplines was not over. So many
ministers look at the structures we have arrived at and, with
no idea of the pain involved, feel that it would be so much
easier to start out fresh and call a new congregation into existence around a different understanding of church. They feel
that in their own denominations membership has been confused with discipleship and that a tremendous pressure is
exerted to increase the number of members. "Being the
church," said one young minister, "means doing something to
bring more people in. Success is not measured in faithfulness
but in how many names are on the rolls."

It is certainly an extraordinarily difficult thing to fight for
integrity of membership within existing structures, but there
is hardly any path that frees one from that struggle. There is
in all of us something powerful at work which seeks to re-
make the new concepts into the old. "Community" can
quickly be changed into "conformity," and "call" into "duty."
I like the line in Exodus that says that "God did not guide

them by the road . . . that was the shortest; for he said,
'The people may change their minds when they see war before them, and turn back to Egypt.' "* It is so easy to turn
back to the old when conflict threatens the peace.

And then there is the old monastic cycle: devotion produces discipline, discipline produces abundance, and abundance destroys discipline. The cycle moves inexorably on and
tremendous effort is required to break its pattern when we
come to the place where discipline is sliding.

Our own time of terrible crisis came in October of 1969.
On the third Sunday of that month, for the first time in the
twenty-two years of the church's history no one stood up to
make his or her commitment. We did not follow the tradition of annually renewing our covenant because the fourth
discipline, "Be a vital contributing member of one of the confirmed groups, normally on corporate mission," was in question.

We had had difficulty with this discipline before. In the
spring of 1965 we had held a meeting of the members in
which three persons presented the differing viewpoints. The
first held that participation in a corporate thrust of the
church is important for membership; the second that participation in any kind of small group is acceptable if the
members hold each other accountable for missionary action
in the world; and a third person presented the argument that
membership in any group is not necessary for growth or mission, but that general belonging and participation in worship
and other programs give what is needed. It was felt that these
three viewpoints existed in some measure in the community
and should be fully examined. After several weeks of discussion, the fourth discipline was confirmed; though it was
agreed that exceptions would be made for sickness and for
those who wanted to meet together to deal concretely and

* Exod. 13:17, NEB

creatively with their everyday vocations as mission in the world. No effort was made, however, to cover every possible exception, since it was emphasized that flexibility and openness to the guidance of the Holy Spirit would always be the primary emphasis in any decision, and that we could never insist on simple adherence to the law.

We thought then that the matter had been settled. The real crisis came four years later when we looked one day at our mission group rolls and faced the fact that one-fourth of our members were in no group at all, reflecting a movement out of groups that to some of us hardly seemed of the Holy Spirit. Again, we came together to look at the painful matter of our division. Once more we gave over our congregational meetings to careful consideration of the fourth discipline. Recommitment Sunday was postponed until we arrived at a decision as to exactly what our commitment was to be.

The question was whether a part of all of the congregation would normally be on mission in membership structures which include the inward and the outward dimension. It was obvious that there was a real difference in judgment at this point. Some felt that the inward-outward structure of the mission groups defined the church as a servant people called into existence to be the community for others. Many contended that this was too narrow a definition and that one was often better able to live out one's servanthood in individual mission. To this the cry came back, "Where then is the place of accountability? Where does one grapple with one's own darkness and gifts, struggle with being a person in depth relationships with others? Where does the church embody in her structures what she proclaims from her pulpit?" The reply came: we could contain both emphases and let those who wanted the corporate dimension be in mission groups, and let the others live on a more individualistic basis.

Gordon said decisively that he did not believe that we could contain both viewpoints under the same organizational and institutional roof without seriously blunting and ultimately losing that which has been our peculiar vision. He further said that he did not believe additional dialogue would serve any constructive purpose. He reminded us that we were not at the beginning of a process, but at the end of one which had in effect been going on for four years. He said that he felt that the question was not one of further defining our differences, but the more painful one of deciding what we were to do about our differences. "How do we free those with different calls to be faithful to those calls?"

When the long weeks of anguish were over, the fourth discipline was again reaffirmed. There were at least a half-dozen people who could not make their recommitment that day in late March. Some remain close and dear friends who continue to follow a costly and radical obedience to the Word, as they hear it, and one can only reaffirm that the task for any of us is to do the will of God and humbly to pray the prayer of Thomas Merton, "I do not see the road ahead of me. I cannot know for certain where it will end. Nor do I really know myself, and the fact that I think that I am following your will does not mean that I am actually doing so. But I believe that the desire to please you does in fact please you."

Every religion and every denomination is founded on a vision defined in disciplines that enable a people to move toward that which they see. Most of these disciplines make our own look shabby, but somewhere along the way they have been abandoned. They remain in the books, but are not taken with any seriousness. My guess is that our own experience gives glimpses of what may have happened. Because we do not want to exclude anyone, we bend to everyone's wish and in the end have no style of life which is noticeably different from that of any other grouping of people. We give no one anything to be up against. We have been transformed by the world—not by the secular outside us but by the secular within us, that part that believes so fervently that something can be had for nothing and that we should not have to choose.

What we did at that important juncture in our life was to face the importance of structurally implementing a description of "Who we are." "Verbal assent," said Gordon, "can mean very little. The implementing structures are crucial." We ended up by saying that the members of the church would live out their lives in small groups on corporate mission. To drop out of a mission group would literally be to drop out of membership in the church.

The council as the governing body of the church was reorganized as a "Mission Council," comprised of two representatives from each confirmed mission group, who serve in rotating order for a period of a year. Representatives report to their groups what transpires in council meetings. Any decisions made are binding on the whole membership. When the council determines that an issue is of such nature as to require confirmation by the total membership, a general congregational meeting is called.

ECONOMICS AND MISSION

Since those days call is more often heard. Each year one or two new missions are launched. It is a common practice for us to give our Christmas and Easter offerings to the newest of them, so that it will have seed money. Most of the missions are eventually able to support their own work. However, when the annual budget is planned, the individual groups, having carefully considered their needs, present them to the budget committee. For the first ten years of its life The Potter's House was in the red, and each year received from $5,000 to $12,000 from the general budget. Now it has its own operating budget of $55,000 and is self-sufficient.

Our mission group structures are tougher and more durable because they have had to cope with the financial dimension.

A group responsible for its own finances is not likely to close shop for the summer or to show laxity in ways that it might if someone else were footing the bills. Furthermore, when the money is ours we relate to the whole sphere of economics in a way that would not otherwise happen. This becomes increasingly evident as our missions in the inner city place us in the midst of the poor. We return to our homes at night and feel less easy with our own life styles.

We used to quote statistics that say the United States, with 6 percent of the world's population, consumes more than 30 percent of its consumable resources, while people in Africa, reduced to eating their seed grain, will not be able to plant new crops. We would state these figures and ask, "How can the Christian community live with those facts?" Today the question has become more personal and less comfortable, "What do those facts mean to me?"

EVERYONE'S GIFT COUNTS

Once a group has come into existence, we struggle with naming the gifts of the members—a concept that is covered by Gordon in his sermon on "The Four Dimensions of the Church." Among the persons touched by its mission the group will again be engaged in the calling forth of gifts. We asked Mrs. Henry, who is in our dinner program for the aged, "What would you like to do?"

"Nothing," she replied. "Nothing is what I want to do. For forty years I left home at 6:00 in the morning and traveled by streetcar and bus so that I could get to my place of work and have breakfast on the table by 7:30. I cooked three meals a day for that family, did their washing and cleaning, and reared their children. When I finished their dishes at night I went home and had to do for my own family. No I don't plan to do nothing but sit, and sit, and sit. I never want to work again."

Evoking the gifts of those who live in the inner city asks

something different of us. Mrs. Henry will not easily believe that her gifts of mind and spirit are needed in the liberation movement. Like so many thousands of the urban poor, she left her rural home as a young person to pursue the promise of work and a better life in the city. Now she does not believe in much of anything. She does not think about salvation for herself or for anyone else. Vast numbers of the poor, however, have a different attitude. They have a growing consciousness of their right to participate in the working out of their own destiny, and are forcefully, sometimes angrily, presenting their claims. Others, deprived of opportunity for creativity, initiative, and space in which to move and rest, experience the rage, frustration, and despair that generate crime.

If the listening to call and the exercising of gifts are unfamiliar concepts in our middle-class congregations, they are stranger still to those in the inner city where choice so seldom exists. And yet, the calls to which we now respond are not issued from our pulpit. They are sounded by the oppressed on the streets of the city, in tenement buildings and rat-infested alleys. By their very presence the poor ask that we do more than "sit, and sit, and sit." "Hear, you who have ears to hear, what the Spirit says to the churches!"*

As new missions come into existence to work with families in the restoring of slum dwellings, to help adults and children learn to read, and the young to develop their leadership skills, some of us who have been on the periphery of the life in our own congregation, together with some of the "third world" of our city, are able to move in closer to the places where new life is breaking. Some days as we labor together, the very climate is alive with possibility, and we begin to feel that we can all believe in ourselves again, and in the power of the Spirit at work in the world.

Perhaps one of these days we who are city dwellers can give

* Rev. 2:11, NEB.

up the myth of our powerlessness, turn around, and move in a new direction. Andrew Heiskell, Chief Director of Time, Inc., said in a recent speech, "For every Federal program designed to rebuild cities, there has been another program equally big that has worked to destroy cities. The highway program, for example, has consistently been the foe of all those who have sought to rebuild cities. The Federal Housing Administration's program destroyed the tax base of most cities by chasing the middle classes to privately owned houses in the suburbs." He was not saying that the cities do not need federal help, lots of it, in terms of dollars, but that government alone could not do the job. "We must learn to manage our society and that means, in good part, managing our cities. If we are to remain a democracy, we must build a society of responsible, self-disciplined individuals. We must devote our minds, our time and our money to that goal, rather than believing that every problem can be resolved by passing another law."

We are beginning to know this. We do not have to sit around immobilized, waiting for help to come. We can join with all the forces of liberation—the small communities that are here and there lighting up the city.

In the neighborhood where I live a group of young people run a cooperative called Stone Soup. By living together and pooling their resources they are making available, at a minimum profit, fresh vegetables, cheeses and other products. Underlying the enterprise is a crazy idea—or is it a human one?—that people ought not to have to pay to eat. Stone Soup takes its name from the legend of two travelers who fed themselves and a whole town a delicious soup they made.

"What are you doing?" a woman asked of the two travelers.

"Fixing stone soup. All you need is a little water and some stones," one replied.

"Of course, it would be better if we had just a bit of potatoes," said the other.

"I have some," she said, and going off, shortly returned with them.

Others passed and stopped to question the strangers. Each time the two travelers explained, and each time the towns-people volunteered to provide the necessary ingredient. At the end of the day every imaginable vegetable, herb, and spice had been added to the pot. That night the two travelers fed the whole town on the most delicious soup anyone had ever tasted.

This legend is reminiscent of another story about fishes and loaves, and deep away in us is a self that knows that this is what miracle is. If it is to happen in the city and in the world we simply have to commit our own human and financial re-sources. We have to recover our own gifts of faith and hope and endurance, evoke the gifts of other persons, and thus develop leaders and facilitators for the building of a global network of small, disciplined, self-critical groups whose reflec-tion will issue in purposeful action. This is a way to be in on the liberation movement that is going on in all the poor countries of the world. We cannot initiate this movement. Even the suffering ones of the earth are not the initiators, though they are the genuine leaders. This movement is God's. He firmly established that when he directed Moses to tell the people that he had indeed seen their misery, and heard their outcry. "I . . . have come down to rescue them from the power of Egypt, and to bring them up out of that country into a fine, broad land . . ."*

In our own congregation the small groups now number over twenty. They are an integral part of the structures that Gordon Cosby has helped to form and that have, in turn, formed him. Although his life is given to working with all the small groups, he is a member of only one, subject to its covenant, under the

---

* Exod. 3:7–8, NEB.

authority of those whose gifts have been confirmed, his heart and mind enlarged and stretched by commitment to the few. He is sometimes advised that his ministry would be increased if he divided his time equally among all the groups, but he remains unconvinced. He believes too passionately that strong leadership is available with all of the groups, and as he moves deeply into the life of one of them his own growth in love is made possible. He is, however, always available to any group as guide and counselor. He is sometimes called in at points of crisis to be a reconciler. He has also worked with many of the groups in the early stages of their formation when they were initially defining the strategy of their mission.

A GLOBAL COMMUNITY

At present a part of Gordon's time is given to helping the Polycultural Institute mission group bring into existence small communities of concerned people all over the world, who will be on both an inward and outward journey. The communities will be very much like our own mission groups. They will, however, be polycultural, reflecting as nearly as possible the diversity found in the Institute itself, where a majority of the students will be drawn from other countries and cultures. We are beginning to look anew at that first Pentecostal community on which the Holy Spirit descended, and wonder why we never noticed before how polycultural it was. Each community will work with meditation, reflection, and study materials provided by the Institute. Consideration will be given to complex global problems such as food and energy shortages, massive poverty, overpopulation, war, and worldwide inflation, so that anyone who really wants to grapple with these issues will have the necessary structures, help and companionship to do so. No one will have to feel alone. Though we are dispersed to the ends of the world, we can begin to identify each other, work together, and even have those times when we come together to meet as one body.

The mission structure gives us a people to companion us in our individual freedom movement. Everyone has extremely difficult struggles to break away from the oppressive inner structures that make us all prisoners of one kind or another. We need a people to journey with us out of our own Egypt into that broad land that is promised to all who believe in Him. "The Son will make you free." The expression of our own freedom will, in the end, be the only credible statement that each of us makes on freedom. Some will be freed for work in ghettos, others to strive for justice in county jails, in halls of government, on boards of industry, or in the writing of a poem.

ART AND MISSION

We have one mission that calls itself The Alabaster Jar. It is made up of people who write and sculpture and paint. Those of us who labor out of guilt or to satisfy some inner Pharaoh ask what all that "entertainment" has to do with mission and the liberation movement. "After all, we, too, could do a little painting if we did not have the poor so much with us." While it is true that not many artists have made profound statements on social issues, this may be because we have not allowed them to live in the midst of the people of the God of the freedom movement. It is so much easier to believe in what one can see, and anyway, who really can know what an artist does with all his or her time? Moreover, artists forsake themselves for fear they are betraying the community. I have a friend, a photographer, who says that sometimes when she has spent long hours in the darkroom she is seized with a panicky feeling, "What if there is no one there when I open the door?" I have kindred thoughts when I have done a piece of writing over a long period of time. I open my eyes and observe that life has gone on without me, and there is the dread feeling that never again will I be able to be "in on" things.

By its very name, The Alabaster Jar group tells us it is all right to follow call even when one is full of self-doubt and is troubled about wasting a "one-time life." They remind us that we do not have to turn out to be another Picasso or Solzhenitsyn—that we are not called to be successful. Rather, we are called to be faithful and to have a contemplative relationship with the ground of being. There is no way to know when one will be used, or how, or what one's life will count for in the long run. The young Pablo Casals, while pouring his life energy into long hours of practice on the cello, could not guess that when Franco came to power, he would stop playing for three years, and that the silence would be heard throughout Spain as if the streets were full of demonstrators. And then, not every artist is called to take up a social or political cause. When the need for bread is met we discover that we have other hungers, and none so deep as the hunger to be understood. The artist helps us to interpret, understand and communicate feeling. When the artist is successful we are led into communion with ourselves and with the world, and it is for want of this that we perish. The solitary work becomes a communal work.

IMPLEMENTING MISSION STRUCTURE

Despite their diversity in outward form, all the missions are ways of casting nets. Ministers struggling with renewal in their own congregations often ask Gordon Cosby, "If you were in a conventional church situation, what would you do to structure the congregation for renewal?"

He usually answers, "What I am doing now. I would preach Sunday after Sunday on my understanding of the nature of the church. I would preach to the limit of my vision—put into words what it is that I see. I would state the disciplines that are essential if one is to have a relationship with the Holy One—God's anointed One, and have one's life changed by him. And then I would sound a call for the mission that has caught my own heart. I would urge others to do the same. After that I would spend the major part of my time just sitting around talking with those who made response to see what would emerge. This sometimes means we let a lot of worthy things go undone."

I put a similar question to the wife of the janitor of the building that we are restoring. "How do you think we can engage the people in this building in the movement to restore the city?" Her response was like Gordon's—"I think we should call them all together and sit around and talk." Now it is our turn to wonder whether we can take the time, for there are no locks on the front doors, the mailboxes are pried open as soon as they are fixed, the neighborhood receives its heroin shots in the basement—not to mention the leaking pipes, garbage and roaches.

The woman says in her way what the educator Paulo Friere says in his way: "Critical and liberating dialogue, which presupposes action, must be carried on with the oppressed at whatever the stage of their struggle for liberation. . . . Attempting to liberate the oppressed without their reflective participation in the act of liberation is to treat them as objects which must be saved from a burning building; it is to lead them into the populist pitfall and transform them into masses which can be manipulated."*

Gordon tells ministers that their major difficulty in implementing the small group concept will be in trying to justify the time they give to the encouragement of one little group when there is so much work that could be done. "For most of us," he says, "it seems an unconscionable amount of time. We cannot get hold of the fact that the process is sometimes as slow as it is, and we become discouraged even when real growth is taking place. We have no perspective when we try to envision what it means for a community to come into

---

* Paulo Friere, *Pedagogy of the Oppressed* (New York: Herder and Herder, 1972), p. 52.

existence. We live under the tension of our own expectations and the expectations of those who are sometimes outright hostile because we are spending our time with a group of unlikely souls when we ought to be taking care of the shut-ins, or the youth, or the elderly. Our congregations are not going to take seriously their responsibility, if we ourselves do not take the ministry of the laity with full seriousness."

Another area that Gordon emphasizes in talking with ministers is their need to accept the relinquishment of control. A staff that feels it necessary to be informed about everything and feels it necessary to be in control cannot allow things to just happen. "No matter how large a congregation—four or five thousand members—if kept under central authority, it will always be a very limited operation."

The small group structure is threatening because it generates things to work with for which we have no clear guidelines, but when you think about it, it is not nearly as threatening as a congregation with no shared responsibility and no shared life.

The small group is not the discovery of Gordon Cosby, or of anyone else. Christ gave us this model. It was he who had the first mission group. He chose twelve. He sent them out by twos. He stayed with them for three years when he must surely have been tempted to add to the little band, to subdivide, and thus to increase the scope of his ministry. Intuitively rather than consciously Gordon has followed this model. A mission group is not brought into existence without a spiritual director and a moderator. In our School of Christian Living we often feel more comfortable with team teaching. More of us are also coming to believe that any group that stays together for less than a three-year period can make neither marked progress in its inward journey nor significant strides toward fulfillment of its mission in the world.

There was a time when, asked to comment on the success of the groups, Gordon Cosby was quick to say that he had the distinction of having presided at the burial of more small groups than had any other minister in the country. Today he would have less reason to make such a claim, for the death of a group is a less frequent occurrence. Groups still go out of existence for varied reasons: when the work is accomplished; when a new form or organization is needed; when leadership does not emerge in sufficient strength; or when the Spirit with its unifying force is absent. Over the years, however, a structure for corporate mission has been evolved that nurtures the inwardness of the group members and, at the same time, enables each one in the group to exercise his or her gift of leadership. The result is a deepening and expanding of the ministry of the group.

MANUAL FOR MISSION

In this handbook are gathered together illustrations of practices that are common to the groups. Until now Gordon Cosby has been—and continues to be—too concerned with the embodiment of Logos in the community to give much attention to the binding of words into books. We would not have this manual were it not for the insistence of his friends here and in other places who feel that the procedures and principles that are being followed could have a universal application. Here Gordon has stated and brought them together in abbreviated form. One might wish for more from him, but perhaps the weakness of the book is in the end its strength, for in giving us only the "nuts and bolts" of small group life, it forces us to fill in from our own experience and to struggle for our own answers.

Those who have watched the proliferation of small groups in our community, often ask, "How do you keep it all together?" Although there is a sense in which no one ever tries, the handbook does give hint that there is reliance on something more than what Bonhoeffer called "cheap grace." One can discern the steel girders under what may appear to the casual eye to be an amorphous out-of-hand, uncontainable, unpredictable sprawl of highly individual cell life.

Occasionally the size or strategy of a given group makes advisable the development of an autonomous structure with new lines of accountability, so that the group maintains only spiritual ties with the entity which we call The Church of The Saviour. So far as Gordon Cosby is concerned, no one structure is sacrosanct. The church, wherever it is, must always be imaging and working with new structures that will enable its members to grow to wholeness in Christ, and to be in the world as a servant people. He proclaims the gospel that only through death can there be rebirth: "The Christian must always think in terms of death and resurrection. The church through its small groups can again be vulnerable in the world. It can take the shape of the suffering servant. We are not to protect ourselves with our own power structures—structures so strong that the world cannot crucify us."

The structures for mission are simple, but through them the Christian message is being rediscovered. Through them Gordon Cosby shepherds a people in the meaning of church. Through them a people learn that there is balm in Gilead, that wounded lives can be drenched with healing, and that the implementation of the Christian gospel means working for justice in the world.

PART ONE

HANDBOOK
FOR MISSION GROUPS

Introduction

Some who visit The Church of The Saviour have honest problems with our approach. Others who come sense the presence of the Spirit in our midst and wonder at the depth and extent of our mission. Most have read Elizabeth O'Connor's books, which describe the various dimensions of our life. Their remaining questions have to do with group structure. Structure, though uninspiring to many, is the key to whether a quality of life shall continue and be made available to others.

The possibilities for the explosion of spiritual power into the world are unlimited. The principles and structures for the release of this power are deceptively easy to grasp, but they are costly beyond description to embody. In this chapter, I have sought to outline certain elementary understandings that we deem to be the critical basis of the mission group experience of The Church of The Saviour.

I.
Handbook
for Mission Groups

WHAT IS A MISSION GROUP?

A mission group is a small group of people (five to twelve) conscious of the action of the Holy Spirit in their lives, enabling them to hear the call of God through Christ, to belong in love to one another, and to offer the gift of their corporate life for the world's healing and unity.

THE INWARD JOURNEY

If a mission group has the capacity to continue to hear the call of God, to deepen its belongings in Christ, and to give its life in mission, it will of necessity be engaged in an inward journey. The following are the minimal dimensions of this journey:

Growth in the life of meditation and contemplation rooted in the Scriptures. This movement will deepen one's capacity for adoration, praise, gratitude and the ability to discern God's will. *Search for Silence* by Elizabeth O'Connor* spells out the vision of this dimension of our life and provides useful exercises for a group.

* Word Books: Waco, Texas, 1972.

Growth in self-understanding. Each of us comes to adulthood severely wounded. This journey into self provides new awareness of the wounds and blockages which keep us from the adoration of God and the giving of ourselves unreservedly to one another. There is always the need for a continuing exploration of the dark and light dimensions of our lives. The search for our inner treasure must never cease. *Our Many Selves* and *Eighth Day of Creation* by Elizabeth O'Connor* provide illumination and specific exercises for this area of growth.

Growth in community. What facilitates community? What blocks community? How belong to others in unlimited liability? How move from being an individual associated with others toward being a corporate person? How build institutions of caring?

The Outward Journey

The mission group by its nature as church is engaged in an outward journey. This is not dissociated from the inward. The true church is always at that juncture where the will of God and the will of the world meet. Because of our inward journey, we can be in the Spirit at that point, serving as the presence of the kingdom. This will be a ministry of presence, service and verbal witness.

The outward journey is possible only as an expression of the inward. Unless the inward issues in the outward, the effort turns in on itself and destroys its pilgrims.

Necessity of Specific Disciplines

The dimensions described above will remain concepts alone unless specific *minimal* disciplines are clearly spelled out and embraced by each member and intern member. The minimal

---

* *Our Many Selves* (New York: Harper & Row, 1971). *Search for Silence* (Waco, Texas: Word Books, 1972).

disciplines are not aspirations. They are not goals to work toward. They are serious commitments to be struggled with daily.

Although minimal disciplines will be spelled out for anyone entering the group, it is imperative that each member and intern member work out his own personal *maximum* disciplines suited to his own condition and pace. Because the members of any group are at various points of development in their lives, the common minimal disciplines are inadequate for effective growth. Failure of each member to work at the appropriate maximum discipline accounts in part for so many groups agonizing year after year and failing on the minimal disciplines.

ACCOUNTABILITY

A group needs to work through a procedure whereby each member will be held accountable for the commitment he or she has made and the disciplines each has embraced. Many groups have found a weekly written report helpful. These reports may be given to one designated to receive and respond to them, and may include:

a. How the disciplines have helped me grow, as well as any failure in keeping them.

b. How God has addressed me through the Scriptures.

c. The crucial problems or peak experiences of my life for the week.

Another means of accountability is that of a periodic in-depth verbal report shared with the group.

Unless some procedure of accountability is followed, a substantial number in the group will become lax in their discipline, thus causing discouragement to the few following them and a deterrent to those considering entry into a mission group.

Note: It is hard to find a person who can hold his or her peers accountable without alienating them.

CATEGORIES OF MEMBERSHIP

A mission group may contain an infinite variety of types, temperaments, and ages. In fact, the more heterogeneous the group, the richer the common life. Members of the group, however, regardless of age or background, must have a seriousness of commitment. The nucleus will consist of those fully committed to Christ and to the dimensions of group life described above. These members have put down their weight, made the group their primary community, and under Christ are willing to be responsible for its life and mission. They continue to re-sound the call of Christ around which the group coheres. They hold one another accountable for the disciplines of the group. They evoke the gifts of one another. They are faithful to the group's mission and its infinite expansion. The members are the church receiving the gift of Christ's presence.

A mission group may have a limited number of people (intern members) exploring the secret at the heart of the members' life and desiring to make the Members' Commitment.

The ratio of members to intern members will depend upon a number of factors, such as the spiritual maturity and clarity of commitment of the members, and the depth of the problems of the intern members as they explore a deepened commitment to Christ and the faith community. For some intern members the movement into membership is easy. For others it is stormy and difficult. A new intern member should be received into a mission group as pastoral care is available by the members of the group.

The intern membership category is conceived as of limited duration. It is hoped that within a year or eighteen months the intern member will be drawn more deeply into an understanding of the call to commitment and be ready to make it, or will be aware that the timing is not of God and will withdraw from the group to pursue his life in another structure.

The great danger is that the intern member will find life in the group supportive and meaningful and will want to remain within it, although unable to make the commitment which alone gives power to the group. Often this desire on the part of the intern member is supported by the members who genuinely love their friend, dislike seeing the issue of commitment clearly drawn, and want the support of another person for the demanding tasks of the group. Even one or two such intern members in a group create problems and make it more difficult for clear options to be presented to others. (See the account of the rich young ruler, Luke 18: 18–23.)

The intern member embraces much the same disciplines as the members, though there are a few differences suited to his exploring state. (See V, "The Intern Member's Commitment.")

HOW A MISSION GROUP COMES INTO BEING

In our beginning years we assumed that a group of committed people who gathered faithfully for Bible study, prayer, and the seeking of God's will for their lives would be given their corporate mission. They never were. This is not a fruitful course to pursue. The reason is the great diversity found in any group. The call that comes to be recognized by one person is not the call of another. No one call emerges to which all in the group can respond. To attempt a common task after a group has formed fails to take into account the deep inner responses of the various ones in the group.

Our procedure now is to start with one person or a small nucleus of persons who have heard a call for a specific mission. Then others gather around that call; they gather initially around "call" incarnated in a person or persons. A new group begins with a clearly understood outward journey as well as a commitment to the inward journey. It is crucial that these dimensions be embodied from the very beginning, otherwise the group begins with many general hopes, aspirations, and longings, but is never able to agree on the common task or the specifics of its disciplines. The minimal disciplines are largely set by the original called person, and they grow out of the experience of the larger community of faith. With these givens, clearer options are provided for those interested in group life.

THE SOUNDING OF THE CALL

The person upon whom the Word of God has come sounds the call in a variety of ways. Often in personal conversations within the community he or she discovers another to share the call. The fire of God kindled within his or her own spirit inflames another. The two are given to each other.

The person's call may be shared with the Sunday morning worshiping congregation or with any segment of the community. A number of people may respond or none. If no one responds, the person waits, nurturing his or her own life in Christ and praying for those who can hear. He pursues his call individually, waiting for the moment others can share it with him. If others respond, they begin their life together, evoking one another's gifts, and praying for clarity in hearing God's will as to their mission. If the new group lives and senses God in its midst, it may share its call with the church council to see if it is confirmed by the representatives of the existing mission groups. This serious testing of call is extremely important.

THE EVOLUTION OF THE CALL

The form in which a call is first heard may be very simple, although in terms of conventional wisdom, impossible. It may first be heard as:

Free my children housed in understaffed, crowded institutions.

Rid my city of illiteracy.

Build a polycultural institute that will be a global community.

Pray for my servants in positions of political power.

Feed my hungry.

But as one is obedient new light is given. The implications and ramifications of the call are seen. A simple call faithfully followed takes one into many interlocking systems. There is no limit to the horizons opened to one's gaze. One may begin with three called people with no clearly defined strategy. How insignificant a mustard seed! One may end with fifteen groups each carrying a necessary part of an incredibly complex task affecting the quality of life in an entire area or perhaps the world. The brief descriptions of the FLOC groups will give some idea of this growth.

An important principle: The real responsibility, including determination of strategy, securing of staff, and raising of funds, must be placed squarely upon the mission group embodying the call. This can be done only by discovering and calling forth the gifts of each group member.

THE EVOKING OF GIFTS

When all is said and done, the discovering and nurturing of the gifts of its members remains the primary work of the mission group. The teaching of St. Paul is clear (1 Cor. 12: 1–31; see II, "The Calling Forth of the Gifts"). Each person confessing Christ as Lord, living within the Body of Christ, is given a gift by the Holy Spirit for the upbuilding of the Body. We can even say that the person himself, as his essence unfolds under the power of the Spirit, is gift. He becomes more fully human, more fully Christian. Functions naturally flowing from this new being are recognized. As these gifts are recognized by the member and confirmed by the other members, they are employed for the enrichment of the group's life. If every member has discovered the unique treasure of his or her own being and it is being received by the others, there is tremendous fulfillment and power. The unity of the group consists in the faithful use of the variety of gifts. If even one or two members have not identified their gifts, the problem of envy will be a serious one for the group.

If a member has not identified his gift, that gift is not likely to increase, nor can he be held accountable for its use by his fellow Christians (see the parable of the talents*). The clear identification and acknowledgment of gift brings new responsibility and awareness of judgment. We fear change and are loath to see ourselves functioning at a level of freedom new for us. To see is to risk failure. To see is to begin to change.

It is well for each group to develop its own vocabulary of gifts, beginning with a study of the gifts identified by the primitive Christian community. Then the group needs to develop its own identifying labels. (See III, "The Four Dimensions of the Church.")

Surely in any group, some of the gifts will be exercised primarily in the deepening of the inner life of the group. Other gifts will be exercised primarily in keeping the group aware and faithful to its outward thrust.

Nothing will happen in a group or by the group in the world unless there is a gifted person to do it. In many self-aware groups much time is spent bemoaning what the group is not. The time could be more profitably spent praying down a gifted person to be it and do it.

A WAY OF LIFE

Preparing People for Mission Groups

Being in a mission group is a way of life. Proper preparation for such a life is important. A person needs to move toward

* Matt. 25:14–30.

such commitment at his or her own pace. He needs the opportunity to experience life in community at various levels. Before making long-range total commitments, the prospective member may make short-range, less threatening commitments. One needs understanding concerning the nature of a corporate life in Christ and the opportunity to taste this life before becoming immersed in it. We try to provide these experiences in our School of Christian Living. They come primarily as a result of the assignments and the sharing of the assignments. For instance, if a class is working on the subject of sin, the assignment may be to identify areas of hostility, violence, or anxiety in one's life and share them with the class. If the class is examining death and its meaning, members may be asked to meditate on their own death. If the topic is prayer, specific assignments in prayer will be made. Primarily as a result of the assignments and the sharing, new awareness breaks and change occurs.

After two or more classes in the School of Christian Living, one may become an intern member of a mission group provided she or he completes the remaining required classes. This dual belonging is too demanding for many. Often it is wise to complete the classes and then move into a mission group as an intern member.

LENGTH OF TIME IN A MISSION GROUP

There is no average time for membership in a mission group. One may be in a group for a few months or for fifteen years or longer. Each member is encouraged to be open to God's call on his life. A deepening understanding of God's call and a deepening awareness of her gifts may lead the member into new dimensions of mission in her original group. Her call may be of long duration, even for a lifetime.

Or the member's growth in the Spirit may lead him into other areas of mission. If there is an existing mission group giving itself to this other area of need, he may join that group. His sense of call will be confirmed by his old group as well as the new group. If there is no existing group responding to his new area of interest, he may sound the new call and be the one through whom a new mission group comes into being. The particular missions making up the total mission of the congregation are determined by the calls of the members.

What areas of human need will we be responding to in the future? We do not know. We seek to be obedient to the calls of God as they are given to our members.

THOSE EXCLUDED FROM MISSION GROUPS

Life in a mission group is so different from other life styles that some preparation is normally necessary. To enter a mission group without preparing for it can be harmful. Some preparatory structure must be provided to give training for life in community and an understanding of the premises upon which life in Christian community is lived. Those unwilling to undergo this training are asked to wait until they see the need for this preparation.

Earlier we outlined the dimensions of life in a mission group. Many people need at the moment a group more limited in its scope. For example, some people prefer a prayer group, or a Bible study group, or an encounter group, or an action group. The mission group embodies the varied dimensions of church. It is total in its scope. It is both inward and outward. It requires that we be accountable to Christ and to one another for the totality of our lives. It assumes that we share unlimited liability for one another. If one is not inwardly ready for such a life, the pressures can be destructive. If one is ready, such a group is life-giving.

The existence in a church of many types of groups meeting many types of needs relieves some of the pressures upon a person to move into a mission group before he is ready. A mission group is not for everyone. It is for those who sense Christ's call to belong to such a group.

How a Mission Group Ends

When there are no longer two or more called members in a group and this is recognized, the group may review its history, give thanks for the months or years of its life, and celebrate its death. Often there is an awareness of sin to be forgiven, grief to be healed, and courage needed for the next steps to be taken.

Corporate Identity Crises

The possibility of stormy group identity crises may be lessened by a thorough understanding and application of the principles described. Especially important is that each incoming intern member have a clear understanding of the covenant into which he is entering. There are many forces working to keep the understanding fuzzy, which inevitably causes trouble later on.

However, in spite of every attempt at clarity, some will come into the group who have not internalized its real nature. Some will withdraw when they are aware that their inner call and that of the group are different. But there are others who will feel duped and will want to change the character of the group. Bringing to the surface the feelings of these members will bring the many selves of many members into consciousness. It may be found that there are no called members left. Or the group may be immeasurably strengthened by the suffering it has undergone.

Why So Difficult?

In our introduction, we said that the principles and structures for the release of spiritual power into the world are costly beyond description to embody. It is rare that any serious attempt is made to embody them. The reasons why may now be seen more clearly.

The heart of the matter is call and obedience to that call. The inward journey preparing one to recognize his gifts and hear the call is long and arduous. "The gate is narrow and the way is hard . . . and those who find it are few."*

Central to mission groups is a primary commitment to a corporate life and a corporate mission. This involves an intense focus and a commitment of time and energy to a handful of people; few believe such a commitment to be worthwhile. Gifted people can see obvious results more quickly and experience more ego satisfaction from individual efforts than from building a community. One must be willing to give a lifetime to three or four people if necessary with no guarantee that his expectations will ever be fulfilled.

Finally, any clear call separates as well as joins us in deeper community. It often separates for a time intimate friends and members of a family. Can I hold clearly to my call and respect calls other than my own? Do I know that calls fundamentally different cannot be lived out in the same group structure?

EPILOGUE

The letter of the law kills; the Spirit gives life. It is possible to understand at a certain level and take seriously all that has been said, and yet for nothing life-giving to occur. The application of the principles can be wooden, legalistic, rigidly applied.

A Christian structure exists to free people from their boundness and to provide healing for their wounds. The spirit infusing the preparation for mission and informing the life in the mission groups is all-important. It is a spirit of beauty, joy,

* Matt. 7:14, RSV.

love, celebration, festivity. This is the opposite of grimness. A free person can be flexible. When a norm is clearly held, exceptions, within limits, can be made without losing the norm.

"The harvest of the Spirit is love, joy, peace, patience, kindness, goodness, fidelity, gentleness, and self-control. There is no law dealing with such things as these."* May God grant you such a harvest!

* Gal. 5:22–23, NEB.

PART TWO

SERMONS
TO MISSION GROUPS

The Sermons

In the preceding section I have described the nature and structure of our mission groups.

On Sunday mornings the members of these groups gather with the whole "community." This is central to our unity as a people. Worship describes who we are, and what we are about. The climate is one of faith and expectancy. Often the Holy Spirit is consciously experienced.

In this context, I believe deeply in preaching. Preaching is a vital part of a community's nurture. My sermons grow out of a life lived intensely with this community, and seek to respond to questions raised and problems faced existentially.

This volume deals primarily with structure; thus the selection of the sermons.

II.
The Calling Forth
of the Gifts

Read 1 Corinthians 12.

Every person called by Jesus Christ into his Body is given a gift, and he is to employ it on behalf of the whole Body, thus making it to function smoothly and know richness and power.

THE PERSON AS GIFT

We have accepted the proposition that the unity and maturity of the Body are closely correlated with the multiplicity and variety of the gifts. A congregation cannot be mature if it has only a few outstanding leaders who exercise charisma; the diversity of gifts within the community must be in operation—they must have been discovered. The so-called lesser gifts are as significant and important as those more easily recognizable. The unity and the maturity of the Body are in direct ratio to the diversity or the multiplicity of the gifts and whether each of the members is employing the gifts. But many do not feel they have a gift or that anything they have is really needed.

What was Paul talking about in 1 Corinthians 12? To begin with, each member called by God to belong to the church comes in by an experience that may take place either very suddenly or over a long period, but it is an experience in which he enters into the life and death and resurrection of Jesus Christ. This is the only way one does come into the Body of Christ—he lives his way into it, with all that this implies.

Such a living out of this life effects a change unbelievably radical. Paul says that if a person is in Christ, old things have passed away; all things become new.* He is saying that the whole basis upon which we operate is different. Our values and the way we view life change. Our whole motivational system is new.

First of all, we are freed from the horrible burden of viewing life as demand, as oughtness, as duty, as obligation, and from the unspeakable pressure of trying to meet the demand. Instead, we see life as "gift." To accept, to know the love of Jesus Christ is to see life as gift, to see it as grace, to see it as feast, as banquet, because Jesus Christ is the *gift* of God. Thanks be to God for his unspeakable gift! For God so loved the world that he gave his only begotten son.

Next, we are freed from the unconscious but very constant attempt to make atonement for our inability to live up to the demands which press in on us. Every person knows he or she is not faithful in living up to these demands, and we keep trying to make atonement—often subtly and sometimes in ways not so subtle. Christ comes primarily as Savior, not as Accuser, and to know Jesus Christ is to know him as Savior. The mood of life, when we live our way into the meaning of being saved by Jesus Christ, becomes one of praise, of gratitude, expectancy, freedom, excitement, wonder, newness, and a feeling of "What gift will be bestowed upon me today?" rather than wondering what will be required of one today.

* 2 Cor. 5:17.

All of this is the result of the gift of the Holy Spirit. It takes place in the very deeps of our being. I have a feeling that the people who talk most freely about this new birth are the ones who understand it least. A unique self begins to emerge. That which was there, though imprisoned, begins to break forth. That illusive thing we call the self begins to take shape. That winsomeness which shone through only in spots, recognizable only by those of special discernment, comes through now more strongly, consistently, and visible to many more people.

We become free enough, safe enough, for unique traits (endearing traits that possibly only a discerning parent ever saw, and that have been lost somewhere along the way) to emerge again. That which is essentially ourselves and which got tied up, traumatized, imprisoned, begins to come forth. This new birth does not impose on the personality something that is alien to it; it brings into actuality, into fullness, that which was always there—those sensitive feelings, those yearnings, those tastes, that tenderer dimension of our natures which somehow has always embarrassed us. One day we become aware that we are no longer afraid of that tenderer dimension of our natures. New strengths begin to emerge, new consistencies, new capacities, new humilities. A mysterious new being is being fashioned, and at the heart of this becoming is the divine action. It is a mystery; we call it the Holy Spirit. Jesus Christ is at work and is making us fully human. He is bringing into being the new humanity ready to be a part of the new creation, to live with God eternally.

Christ makes each of us something unlike any other creation ever fashioned by God—something wonderful, exciting, unique; something specifically needed in the total Body of Christ. This uniqueness, this very self that is so hard to describe, this charismatic person, is the gift of the Holy Spirit. It is the primary gift that we bring to the Body, and without it the Body is immeasurably impoverished.

CALLING FORTH THE GIFTS OF OTHERS

Now, since the calling forth of uniqueness is God's mission, it seems self-evident that this is our primary calling as Christians. We are to call forth the gifts of other people, to set them free, to throw the lifeline to them and be the one who, under God, helps a person discover that for which he was created.

The question is, how to call forth the gifts in others? It is amazing how long we can be with people and not call forth any gifts. In fact we often do just the opposite. But to love a person means to help them recognize their uniqueness and to discover their gifts.

In Freedom

I think we begin to be really helpful in calling forth the gifts of others when we understand and employ our own charisma, when we ourselves are functioning in freedom, when our "oughtness" is eliminated and we can have the time of our lives doing what we want to do. The genuineness of our freedom is easily discernible and the element of duty or oughtness is also easily discernible. Children discern their charisma, their uniqueness as it unfolds, when mothers enjoy being mothers and fathers being fathers. They are seeing parenthood as a gift, not as demand. But without the exercise of the charisma of motherhood or fatherhood, the charisma of the child is not drawn forth. One of the difficulties that family life has is too much oughtness, too much demand, too much keeping the machinery going.

The counseling of another is effective only to the extent that we employ this skill in freedom and don't help the other person merely because we feel we ought to. Preaching or teaching are effective when they are free, spontaneous, and cheerful, rather than some sort of exhibitionism. There is

nothing more difficult to bear than a false gaiety and cheerfulness that form a protective coating. But a genuine cheerfulness is a form of faith and is a corollary of the free exercise
of one's own gifts. Jesus says, "In the world ye shall have
tribulation." You are going to be up against all sorts of things,
but "be of good cheer; I have overcome the world."* This
is what he said to person after person. He didn't mean "Cheer
up!" in the superficial, saccharine way we often do. The
cheerfulness he was talking about is a characteristic of a person who exercises his charisma in freedom.

I think all of us had best find out what we really want to
do and start doing it, with whatever it involves. If you have
to give up your responsibility, give it up; if the church goes
to pieces, so be it. But we've got to find what we want to do,
really, because nothing else is going to help anybody.

IN DETACHMENT

In calling out the gifts of others, somehow we'll have to
stop trying to control them. We'll have to learn something
of the meaning of detachment. Joe Knowles, a pastoral counselor with the Pastoral Counseling and Consultation Center
of Greater Washington, tells this story which illustrates detachment. He was running one of his therapy groups when
something began to happen that was very exciting and also
very threatening. Joe started to control the discussion so the
group would work out right and the situation wouldn't get
out of hand. As he was tempted to do this, God spoke to him
and said, "Joe, take your hands off the group." He obeyed
for a few minutes, took his hands off, and let the group continue to move. But he became a bit anxious again and started
to get in there to control it. God spoke to him again and
said, "Joe Knowles, take your hands off the group." For a

* John 16:33, KJV.

few minutes he obeyed, but then he started in again. This time God said, "Joe Knowles, take your cotton-picking hands off that group!" When God speaks in sectional language he's more likely to get through.

We have the feeling that if we do take our hands off—what in the world might emerge? We might not like what would emerge in our husband, or wife, or friends. Our church might become something entirely diffcrent from what it is now. We are afraid to take our hands off, although what we wind up with, what we fashion is hardly worth having. In subtle and overt ways we try to mold others, until our closest friends are in a straitjacket. The Holy Spirit will work if we just release the person and let any sort of strange concoction emerge. It is the hardest thing in the world to release one who is meaningful to us and to stop clutching and fashioning.

In Expectation

God has not created a single person whose essence and uniqueness are not eternally needed. He will keep longing for you and for me and keep reaching out for us; he will keep searching for that one lost sheep until we discover our charisma. The only way we can really take our hands off, when we love a person, is by committing him in a new way to God's care, to God's love. It is being willing to trust God for whatever strange new work may emerge in the person we release.

In the process of gradual release of the person who is being born anew through the power of the Holy Spirit, the real character of the new humanity is obscured for a time by the turmoil, the anxiety, the hostility, the downright hatred which also begin to emerge into consciousness. The true dimensions of the old humanity are seen for what they are. This can be a time of discouragement and despair, when one sees with greater objectivity the unbelievable demonic shadows of one's life, the indifference to the spiritual, one's unwillingness to

take the risk of faith, one's inability to love, and the ease with
which we actually despise our brothers and call them fools
in a thousand subtle ways. But even so the new begins to
emerge, and this "becoming" self is the gift of the Holy Spirit.
It is this new self that is needed by Christ and his Body.
Without it the new humanity, the new creation, will not be
complete. The creation will be forever incomplete without
you, without your gift. This is a staggering truth.

Out of this fundamental gift will emerge perhaps many
gifts. There will be many functions, though they will change
from time to time. There will be motherhood, fatherhood,
teaching, preaching, administration, healing. Then the time
will come when we no longer exercise certain gifts, perhaps
because of illness or old age, but we will still belong to the
Body, and more deeply than we do now, because we are
grafted more deeply into it. The primary thing is the gift
of the person, regardless of his function.

We have said the task and the primary mission of the
Christian is to call forth this gift and these gifts from others
—the gift of the Holy Spirit. This is the Good News. We are
not sent into the world in order to make people good. God
forbid! We are not sent to encourage them to do their duty.
The reason people have resisted the gospel so is that we have
gone out to make people good, to help them do their duty,
to impose new burdens upon them, rather than calling forth
the gift which is the essence of the person himself. We are
to let people know that God is for them. We are to let them
know that they are not doomed to an existence that is less
than fully human. God is calling them into the family of his
love; their uniqueness forms a part of the whole. God is a
gracious God who has already judged the earth in mercy in
Jesus Christ. This is the Good News—that they can be. They
can be what in their deepest hearts they know they were intended to be, they can do what they were meant to do. As
Christians we are heralds of these good tidings.

BECOMING OURSELVES

Why is it so very difficult to call forth another's gift? Why do we so often, after converting a person, make them twice as much children of hell as before?* This is the net result of some of our "evangelism," and Jesus saw this very clearly.

No matter how much we love a person, accept him, give him support, have warmth and affection for him, no matter how much we help him in so many ways, unless we can actually call him forth so that he is himself exercising the uniqueness God gave him, then the love is incomplete; he is not free, he is less than fully human.

We have said that the most effective thing we can do to call forth the gift of another is to employ our own gift in freedom. This may seem selfish at first. Aren't we supposed to help the other person? What does our own gift have to do with it? We start there.

The charismatic person is one who, by his very being, will be God's instrument in calling forth gifts. The person who is having the time of her life doing what she is doing has a way of calling forth the deeps of another. Such a person is herself Good News. She is the embodiment of the freedom of the new humanity. Verbal proclamation of the Good News becomes believable. The person who exercises his own gift in freedom can allow the Holy Spirit to do in others what He wants to do.

Our problem is that we resist God's giving to us his very life, and we also resist receiving the gift of another. It is much easier to love in a moralistic sense, or to do something for another person, than it is genuinely to love and care for the person, to call forth the gift. To call forth another's gift is to love her as she is; to want her to be what and who she is

* Matt. 23:15.

at the given moment, no matter what and who she is. But most often we do not want God—or the essence of the person.

Through Discipline

Our discipline of prayer is a channel by which we receive the gift of God's very being. This is not merely a rule that we keep—it is a time when we get still. It is a time when we let God address us, command us, penetrate us, exercise his sovereign will over us. It is a time when he addresses us and we respond; a time of dialogue, of actually receiving the gift of God. The trouble we have getting to this time of prayer and making this a basic, vital point of our lives says something about our resistance to the gift of God. We say we have trouble with our disciplines, but another way of saying it is that we don't want God to get too close.

For long centuries the people of God have had God speak to them in a unique way through the Scriptures. It is the Living Word of God whereby he actually comes to us—it's not merely the reading of a book, or the keeping of a rule. Why do we have trouble with it? Because we have trouble receiving the gift of God's very life.

This is true of worship, too. It is a time when we are open to the living God. We come to receive him, and no telling what would happen to us if we conceived worship in its proper terms as the time when the living God is present in our midst. Who knows what might happen if we *really* believed this, as a people!

To be part of a fellowship group or a mission group simply means that God speaks to us when we are bound together in a disciplined covenantal community. God comes to us through people, he comes to us through the community of faith. Again, we have trouble at the point of yielding our lives, being obedient to one another.

The discipline of giving is the response to the desperate and poor of the world. It is the symbol of our trust in God's provision for us, it is the opening of the channels so that God can come; we do not hold on to our own security. But again we seem to say, "God, don't come too close."

Through Jesus Christ

Let us keep it clearly in mind that God gives the gift of himself to humanity through Jesus Christ. Our very resistance to Jesus also says something about our fear of God—the gift of God concretely given to us. So often we feel that God the Father and God the Holy Spirit are sufficient; God the Son is a confusing extra. We don't quite know what to do with him. Now it is through Christ that God gives himself to us, and enters into covenant relation with humanity.

It is through the gift of Jesus Christ that the freeing takes place as we accept him. The emerging of our own uniqueness comes as we accept Jesus Christ as Savior and as Lord, as Master. But at this point of concreteness we hesitate, we argue, we wait. In Jesus Christ there is no abstraction which allows us to remain in control of our own destiny. Here is one who comes in the form of a servant, who comes giving his life to the uttermost, who comes dying on a cross. Here is one who comes on our behalf for our reconciliation, as our Redeemer, claiming our total allegiance. He gives himself totally to us and asks that we give ourselves totally to him.

When we are open to this gift, all of life is thrown into a new orbit. We know intuitively that it is a great risk to accept this gift. We know that if we are open to it, if we are open to him who is Sovereign Lord, we shall be profoundly changed. We are not dealing with an abstraction, we are dealing with God who is incarnate in human history, who comes to us as a Person. So we ask the question, What will happen if I do let him come in, if I accept him as Lord? What will I be like when he is done with me?

Through Risk

Now most of us want to change at those points where our present unhealthy responses to life cause us pain. But we want to hold on to much of the way we are put together. If we accept this gift of God, the gift of his own life, we cannot remain what we have been; we will become a new creation. The problem is largely one of willingness to take risk, to let our own images of ourself go, of taking the risk of what will happen when God actually breaks into human life and begins his work down in the deeps of our beings, and not knowing what will emerge, not knowing what we will be, not knowing at all what kind of persons we will become.

Somehow there has to be the faith and the trust that what we will become will be right because God is doing it. It is at this point where the church, when it has been true to itself, has for two thousand years continued to proclaim Jesus Christ as Savior and Lord of life. The church says we must begin with personal acceptance of Jesus Christ; this is where we begin to participate in the new humanity. This is where we start, where we accept the gift of God in the concreteness of his Son.

To resist Jesus Christ is really to resist the very essence of God; it is to resist who and what God is; it is to ask him to be someone he is not. This we do so often with one another —before we accept you, you must be something that you are not; be that which I would like for you to be. We do this to God.

AGAPE LOVE

In all that we have just discussed, we have been trying to come to grips with the nature of love, and we have found it is not as easy as we thought. William Barclay says the word most frequently used in describing Christian love is *agape*. The noun is used approximately 120 times in the New Testament, and in its verbal form, more than 130 times.

Why did the New Testament writers discard the other words for love and use the word *agape* almost exclusively? For one thing, *eros* was used most often in connection with lust. And rather than *philia*, according to Barclay, Christians needed a more inclusive word. *Agape* love demands the exercise of the whole person to all people—to those who are nearest and dearest, to those who love us, to those who are in the Christian fellowship, to neighbor, to enemy, to the world. This kind of love has to do primarily with the mind and with the principle by which we deliberately live; and with the will. It is the power to love the unlovable. It is the power to love people we do not like.

Jesus commands us to love our enemies in order to be like God; not in order to win our enemies or to get results, but that we may be sons of the Father who sends his rain on the just and the unjust, who looks after both the good and the evil.* The predominant characteristic of this *agape* love is that, no matter what a person is like, God seeks nothing but his or her highest good. It is an unconquerable benevolence, an invincible good will. It has to do with an activity of the whole person toward the other person, and with taking the initiative.

Willing the highest good is a very general sort of thing. But it is also specific in that it will provide an atmosphere for other persons to exercise their own uniqueness in freedom so that they become alive. They become fully human and what God intended when he created them. Loving in this sense has to do with the whole way we are put together and the way we respond as human beings. It is not merely something we do as a matter of principle, it is not simply a rule—it is a way of life.

THE UNIVERSALITY OF LOVE

Love has to do with the way we see life and people and their meaning. The Christian sees people betrothed to God through Jesus Christ. This is shocking. God has betrothed himself to *all* humankind regardless of what we are like, so all

* Matt. 5:43–48.

humankind is potentially in Jesus Christ. Each of us can respond, but God is married to us whether we respond or not.
It's ridiculous! It's absurd! The scandal of the gospel!

Agape love is not something which is fitful, or spotty. In
a sense it is not at all selective. How does it use discretion
concerning the particularities of loving? How do I give the
gift of myself? How do I give the gifts which express myself
to a particular person? In this sense love has to use discretion,
but in another sense it is not selective at all; it just reaches
out. It is for every person and for every combination of persons. There is no exclusiveness, no discrimination. The rain
falls on the just and the unjust and God looks after the evil
and the good.

If there are people we are not for—people for whom we
do not desire good, happiness, joy, fullness of being, the fullness of humanity—if there is any combination of people, any
segment of humanity, no matter how cruel and how harmful
one segment is to another segment, how much one segment
is an enemy to other segments of mankind and womankind—
if we are not for all segments and all people, then this agape
has not broken for us.

So often we say, "Yes, I am for him, but . . . ; I am for
her, but . . ." This "but" is more powerfully heard than our
being for the person or willing his good. We will have to
eliminate the "but." "No matter what his problem, no matter
how difficult she is, I'm for this person or this group. I will
affirm, protect, encourage, stand alongside. I shall not be
bothered in the slightest by 'guilt by association' or 'con-
tempt by association' because I stand alongside." Here there
is a close identification with all persons.

THE PARTICULARITY OF LOVE

In addition to the universality of love there is also a particularity, which is important. Certain people are given to us
for a continuing, more costly involvement; we don't select

them. To be with these people in this way, to recognize this givenness, means a much more threatening self-revelation, an opening up in ways that leave us with a sense of awe. In the presence of the inwardness of another, the uncovering of another, we are on holy ground.

It is necessary to have the universality and the particularity in the right creative tension; both are important. The universality must prepare us for the particularity, and the particularity for the deeper thrust into the life of all mankind, else that fatal twist: in loving all mankind we will love no one deeply and in seeking to love one person we will love him or her exclusively and neglect the rest of the human race.

THE RISK OF LOVE

Another aspect of *agape* love also involves faith, and this is the matter of risk-taking. There is no loving without enormous risk. There must be willingness for something to emerge in the beloved that is quite different from what we could predict. It is not given to us to see with any completeness what another will be when his or her gift is fully known or exercised. It is fun employing the imaginative gift, as we reach out in love to another, but the outlines of what we picture must be held rather loosely, because it is God who will call forth unimaginable newness, genuine uniqueness. And who can picture uniqueness which is not yet?

I talked recently to a friend concerning two possible procedures as he made his search for God. One involved participation in the life of this community, its worship and its more formal phases. The other did not involve being a part of this particular church. As we talked, I suggested that either course was all right with me and would not affect my love for him.

"I know you mean that," he responded, "but I can't understand its being all right with you either way."

It has to be all right either way, because we do not know what path really leads to the uniqueness of the person. Part of our difficulty lies at the point of risk-taking. If I love this person unreservedly, if my unreserved love in some way calls forth his gift, will the person give himself to me when he has the whole world to choose from? Perhaps we have chosen each other in great immaturity and mutual need. If this person becomes a free, charismatic person, perhaps I won't be in the running at all. Sometimes the opposite is true, and perhaps he will choose me and I don't want him to choose me. There is no escape from this risk-taking.

Love is a matter of faith in God. I have to know that somehow God is gracious and he can be trusted; he is for me. He can be counted on to "grow me up" into the fullness of the stature of Jesus Christ. He has chosen me, he is for me, and "if God is for us, who can be against us?"* God is faithful and what he is producing in the other person can be trusted not to restrict me. The very act of loving the person is a freeing thing and we need not fear what God will do to us through the other.

THE SACRIFICE OF LOVE

Love is two things: it is seeing and risk-taking. But there is a further issue that is very important—the transition from not loving to loving, from being powerless to call forth the gift of another to becoming the channel of this miracle, where aliveness occurs in another because God loves through us and reaches into the deeps of another through us. What is in this transition? What does it involve? The assumption we usually make is that if the person is loved she will be loving; if he has been made secure he will make other people secure. We assume that the more love a person receives the more he has to give, and the more security she has, the more she can be depended on to give others a sense of security.

Dr. Peter Bertocci, professor of philosophy at Boston Uni-

* Rom. 8:31, TEV.

versity, seriously questions this sequence. There is a deeper question to consider here, he says. When I receive love, or understanding, or security, I am a relatively passive participant. The other person is doing the thinking, the imagining, the giving, the actual loving. He or she is experiencing whatever creativity is involved. If I am to move from being loved to loving, a different orientation is called for, one involving action, the willingness to sacrifice, to be misunderstood for the sake of another's good. This transition from being loved to loving is radical and calls for a new conception of myself. How does this happen? And what is it that happens? The essence of it is an emotional experience of knowing Jesus Christ.

The Source of Love

How do you let Jesus Christ in? How does he begin to talk with you? He is the source of the love; you simply can't do this kind of loving on your own; it's not natural! Loving involves faith, and our relationship with Jesus Christ who is the gift of God's love. This is what Holy Communion is all about—receiving the gift.

Don't let anything stop your seeking this personal, intimate relationship with this Person, Jesus, with all your heart and mind and soul. This is the key. This is the only explanation that I can see to this transition from being loved to loving. Some of us have been greatly loved through the years and we still don't know how to love this way. Some of us had security, as much as people normally ever have, and we still don't spend our lives giving other people security. Then there are some people who haven't had any security at all. There are some who haven't been loved. Yet they are able to give love in a way that they have never humanly received it, because of this strange miracle that takes place within the human soul—the miracle of a living relationship with Jesus Christ.

III.
The Four Dimensions
of the Church

Read 1 Corinthians 12, 13, 14.

THE FOUR DIMENSIONS OF THE CHURCH

Some new directions and emphases are becoming clearer in the life of the congregation of The Church of The Saviour. There is a new awareness that life as it is lived out in our mission groups has come to be characterized by four dimensions and that these dimensions are essential if the church is to be fully and completely the church of Jesus Christ.

CHANGE

The first of these has to do with the church as the area of fundamental change. To belong to the church of Jesus Christ is to become part of a community whose very purpose is to nurture its members in such a way as to bring about a transformation of life. It is assumed that a person who seeks membership is willing to undertake a difficult inner journey. Like the Psalmist he will frequently be in dialogue with himself. "Why are you cast down, O my soul, and why are you disquieted within me? Hope in God."* He will wonder why he is dissatisfied with himself, why he is so depressed. He

* Ps. 42:11, RSV.

86

will descend to the depths within to grapple for insight—for a new awareness of that which has been hidden within the unconscious.

Such a person will also be in continual dialogue with God so that what she becomes increasingly aware of within herself may be brought to God for healing. There will be repentance and waiting upon God. But that which she seeks will be much more than an increased awareness or a heightened sensitivity to her own imperfections. She will be weighed down by a sense of desperate need for that fundamental change that makes possible the healing of sin.

The anguish involved in becoming aware of the depths of one's own sinfulness is dealt with in a very helpful way by Thomas Merton in a book entitled *Contemplative Prayer*.* He describes that experience of dread, nothingness and night in the heart of man which arises out of "awareness of infidelity to the truth of life."

The problem with many of us is that as yet we have not even reached the point in our spiritual development where we know what Merton is talking about. In the community of faith the supernatural grace of Jesus Christ is mediated to us in such a way that we become aware of ourselves as sinners, and recognize our need of healing. The self is surrendered; a fundamental change takes place. This is the first dimension of the Christian church. It is a laboratory of change.

WITNESS

In its second dimension the church is to be thought of as a people who witness with clarity to the Power which can produce this change. This Power can forgive sin, transform our society, renew our cities, make our nation new, change its priorities, and bring newness into the life of the world. Because it has self-consciously entered into that life and into

* New York: Doubleday Image Books, 1971.

that Power, the church can name the Name—can proclaim to all its undivided loyalty to Jesus, through whom all life can be reborn.

Some question the wisdom of naming the Name, of publicly acknowledging Jesus as Lord and God. There are those who declare that it is inadvisable to do so, for fear of alienating those to whom we would speak of the gospel. The strange thing is that the world is much freer in expressing its hunger and its desire for God than the church, which has come to be very reluctant to use spiritual terms.

There are many reasons for this. There has been so much inauthenticity in the church that sometimes to name the Name can be tremendously alienating. But if there is authenticity in the life of a church, the world will not be alienated by the bearing of witness; in fact, the only way we can have any genuine dialogue with the world is clearly and emphatically to name the Name and to be outwardly what we are inwardly. If other people want to know me, they have to know me as a man in Christ, because this is who I am. If anyone really wants to know this community, they have to be in dialogue with a community that is what it is because it is in Christ.

The mission groups of The Church of The Saviour—the nurturing, serving communities of which our church is composed—must be, first and foremost, places where one can clearly bear witness to the Power that is the only power, the Name that is the only name, in which life can become new, and so be forgiven. We are a witnessing people. "If the trumpet give forth an uncertain sound, who will prepare himself for the battle?"* No wonder it is so difficult to make the transition into the community of faith, into all it costs to surrender life to Jesus Christ! The witness is so often dim and the sound blurred. It is better to run the risk of speaking the Name even though the authenticity is not as clear as we

---

* 1 Cor. 14:8, KJV.

would like it to be, than it is to be hesitant in naming the Name.

NURTURE *must happen or others won't*

In its third dimension, the church, this witnessing people, must also be a nurturing people. It is of crucial importance that every mission group should be able and eager to nurture and shepherd anybody whose life is awakened and who wants a shepherding relationship, who wants to move from where he is in his hunger and his interest to the place where he is confronted by the kerygma, by the demands of the gospel. Likewise the group must be able to give guidance and inspiration to anyone who, having already been confronted by Christ and having responded in faith, is eager to move on to that stage where she will be stabilized in the faith, will grow into maturity in it and discover her gift of the Holy Spirit. Every such person ought to have a nurturing community willing to shepherd them in their spiritual development.

It is difficult for people to find this sort of shepherding. People literally travel around the world and are unable to find it. Yet the church of Jesus Christ is to be a nurturing community, a shepherding community that will always reach outside itself to provide direction and encouragement for anyone who wants it, not demanding that they come into the community of faith before they are ready to make the commitment such a life demands.

ACTION

The fourth dimension of the church, and of our groups, is that of action. Not just any action, but Christian action. This means that the group will take on some segment of the pain and the hurt of mankind and will in the name of Christ go out to it for its healing. While it is acting it will also be a people who are bearers of the Holy Spirit. It will engage in intercessory prayer for the healing of the world's hurt, and it will bring vision—the vision that all of mankind is one, and that one day all of mankind will be consciously in the love of God, brought to its uniqueness and to its fullness of life. This is the vision, for the lack of which the people perish. This vision enables people to see that life will be different because God is God.

Obviously, to belong to the church is very difficult because it always involves these four dimensions of existence. There are many people who would like to join a group with one or two dimensions, but not all four. Many want some sort of self-engagement, but they don't want God-engagement. They will be under pressure if they are in a group that is clearly committed to both. Others want to get in on the action: "Let's get on with it. Let's do the job. Let's don't sit around. That's the trouble, we've been engaged in too much of this God business. Now let's get on with the task." These people will be very uncomfortable in a group where there is serious self-engagement and serious God-engagement. However, the church of Jesus Christ involves these four basic dimensions, and if the group is faithful to its Lord, it will always seek to deepen those dimensions so that a person can grow into fullness of life.

THE GIFTS OF THE SPIRIT

How can this transformation of life take place? The New Testament answer to this question is that we are to take seriously the evoking of the gifts of the Holy Spirit. This is the only way in which a group can move with power in these four dimensions. Our conviction is that there is an essential quality of life, different from that of the purely human and transcending it. There is a whole new realm of power that was released in the Resurrection and which broke into human life at Pentecost. This power can flow into our lives. As we confess faith in Jesus as Lord, we confess that we are sinners. This opens the way for the power to transform our lives. Increasingly we come to know life in the Holy Spirit and to rest in it. We begin to know the peace that passes all understanding. We begin to surrender the self so that it is not struggling for power against God and against other people. We are in a new realm. "If anyone be in Christ Jesus, he is a new creation. Old things have passed away. All things have become new."*

Then to each of us a gift is given by the Holy Spirit for the upbuilding of the Body so that it can give itself for the healing of mankind.

In his first letter to the Corinthians, chapters 12 and 13, Paul speaks of the great variety of spiritual gifts, emphasizing the fact that "to each is given a manifestation of the Spirit for the common good," and that the Spirit "apportions to each one individually, as he wills." In other words, the gift conferred by the Holy Spirit upon the new person in Christ is not a vague, general propensity, but a specific power or capacity peculiar to an individual, to be exercised for the good of the group. The failure to take this teaching of Paul seriously is the cause of the apathy and ineffectiveness in the Christian church of our time.

These specific spiritual gifts are received only when the church is the church as Christ intended it to be, that is to say, when it is made up of relatively small groups of people characterized by intimate, close relationships, and committed to a specific mission directed toward winning some small corner or segment of the world for Christ. In the mission groups of The Church of The Saviour we are experiencing an impressive demonstration of the emergence through the power of the Spirit of an amazing variety of specific new gifts and capacities, each directed toward the building up of the group and the carrying out of its objectives.

* 2 Cor. 5:17.

THE PRIOR

First there is the gift of those capacities that need to be exercised in each group by the person who is called the Prior. This is a term taken over from our Catholic fellow Christians because we could think of no other half as good. The Prior is much more than a mere moderator; he or she is the shepherd of the shepherds in the group. He is the overseer of the little flock. He is the one who, under the Chief Shepherd, assumes responsibility—final responsibility—for this people that has been given to him by Jesus Christ, and who knows that one day he will present this flock to the Chief Shepherd. He loves the flock and intercedes for it in something of the spirit of Jesus, who interceded for his little flock, saying, "Father, here they are and only one is lost, the son of perdition. I only lost Judas."* In these words one feels the agony, the love of Jesus, as he presents his flock to his Father.

The Prior prays that every single person within the group will come to the fullness of his own unique capacities, will discover his gift of the Holy Spirit, and therefore will have the sort of power with which it is possible for a person to move into the future. The Prior's responsibility is to see that each person is exercising a gift on behalf of the group. If any of the roles should be unfilled, he will fill them as best he can on an interim basis. If there is no administrator, he will be the administrator. If there is no shepherd, he will be the shepherd. He will see to it that the various gifts within the life of the group complement one another.

THE SPIRITUAL DIRECTOR

The second of the newly emerged gifts in our mission groups is that of the Spiritual Director, another term taken

---

* John 17:12.

from Catholic literature but used by us in a less formal, more mutually directive sense. The responsibility of the Spiritual Director is to work out that optimum structure of discipline, study, and personal devotion which shall best further the spiritual growth of the individual members of the group and of the group as a unit. It is also his or her function to see to it that the members are faithful to this structure; he or she has been given authority by the group to hold them accountable. Thus is provided an arrangement which resists that almost inevitable tendency in any small group to reduce itself to the lowest common denominator of study and growth. The deepest spiritual sensitivity available in the group is enlisted in the effort to provide an environment and a discipline that shall be conducive to growth and to a transformation of life into the fullness of the stature of Christ. This is an indispensable element in every group.

Experience has shown that this arrangement for the maintenance of accountability in the group is greatly assisted by the practice of journal keeping. At the end of each day—or, as some prefer, at its beginning—each member of the group notes in a spiritual journal the significant events and illuminating thoughts of the day. As she has endeavored to walk with Christ in his Way, what have been the insights to be treasured for tomorrow? What are the pitfalls to be avoided? What were the friction points in her effort to subject her life to discipline? What did Christ say to him as he was in dialogue with Christ through the Scriptures? What are the personal and social issues he is struggling with? At the end of the week, just before the group meeting, each member summarizes his experience in a one-page report which he submits to the Spiritual Director. On the basis of these records, if they are perceptively written, the Director learns to know the individual and group mind and spirit, and the needs of the fellowship, in a way not otherwise possible. This is what is

meant by "accountability," as an invaluable aid to bringing
the totality of life under the lordship of Christ.

THE PASTOR-PROPHET

A third gift of the Spirit essential to the spiritual well-being
of the group is the ability to carry out the function of Pastor-
Prophet. This person, on a day-to-day basis, actually nurtures
the people within the flock. He or she stays in touch with
them, makes them feel that there is someone who cares, and
is in touch at the point of crisis, or in celebrations. When
they are sick or grieving, he is there. He is there with something of the gentleness and meekness of Christ. "Take my
yoke upon you, and learn of me; for I am meek [gentle] and
lowly in heart: and ye shall find rest unto your souls."* She
is the kind of person who can help people find rest for their
spirit, who can encourage them. But in addition he or she is a
prophet who has the capacity to help people see the will of
God for their lives now. He speaks forth the word of God, he
helps with the unmasking process, he helps to produce crisis
in that he helps people to engage in self-criticism and to see
those areas where they are unsurrendered. He confronts a fellow member where that member needs confronting.

It is necessary that one individual should be both Pastor
and Prophet. People tend to seek out the person who embodies the pastoral function—who encourages them, who
treats them with gentleness and loving concern. But they
likewise tend to avoid anyone who embodies the prophetic
function—who deals with them sternly, when need be, ad-
mitting no evasion or compromise. The Prophet speaks in
love but insists on the truth being faced. Thus if both these
functions are embodied in one individual, there can be no
playing off the one against the other. However, it is a great
responsibility of the Pastor-Prophet to avoid his or her own
inner ambivalence in these matters.

* Matt. 11:29, KJV.

THE SHEPHERD

Another gift of the Spirit manifested in our mission groups is the ability to be a Shepherd. The Shepherd—and there may be more than one in a group—is a person who has undertaken the responsibility on behalf of the group, for the sake of Christ, of giving guidance and instruction to those who have expressed interest in the group but are still outside. Some such people are little more than kindergarteners in the faith. But it is amazing how fast they can mature under the guidance of a good Shepherd. Our group experience has demonstrated that in a few weeks, under the counseling of a Shepherd who is really an undershepherd of Jesus Christ, a soul can develop a lasting enthusiasm and sense of direction and can begin to assume responsibilities in connection with the mission of the group as he moves toward confrontation with Christ and total commitment.

OTHERS

In addition to the four gifts mentioned as essential, there are others that may minister to the life and purposes of the group. For instance, there is always a wide field for the special capacities of the Ecumenist, who keeps the group in touch with many other combinations of Christian life, both within his own church and within other churches. He or she contributes to the maintenance of unity and mutual understanding among the many groups in his own church and brings his own Christian community into the ecumenical stream of a worldwide fellowship. As a result, wherever group members go, they meet people to whom they are known and whom they know in the Spirit; they become part of a community which spreads out, not only in space and time, but beyond—the Church Triumphant as well as the Church Militant.

Every group needs at least two or three Activists—individuals who, impelled by the Spirit, help the group to take on more and more of the pain and the hurt of mankind. The group needs to be reminded that it has constantly to extend itself, and that it is by definition a people of vision and of presence. Likewise the group has need of those who will undertake the special function of the Evangelist and the Apostle, to be agents of the group in new, and perhaps alien territory, there to present the claims of the kerygma in such a way that others may not be alienated but may respond.

It is important to keep clearly in mind that responsibilities must be specific. Armored with gifts of the Spirit, along lines suggested in the preceding discussion, a group will have three individuals who are specifically charged with the internal life of the fellowship: the Prior, the Spiritual Director, and the Pastor-Prophet. It will have one or two gifted individuals, the Shepherds, who are always focused on people outside the group, with the purpose of bringing them to the place where they are ready to make some sort of commitment when Christ calls them. It will have people who are always pushing the group out into new dimensions of activity. Altogether it will have all the gifts of the Spirit embodied in people whose responsibilities are clearly focused and defined. When these are not clear and accepted as being of the Spirit, there is no accountability. This is one of the reasons we are prone to keep the gifts vague and general.

Recently on retreat I watched a person struggle with a call to be a Shepherd. She had been resisting it, although she had been a Christian for many years. Finally she came to the place of saying, "Yes, I will accept this gift; I want to be a shepherd. This is what Christ is calling me to be; now, God, send me my first sheep." There is all the difference in the world between just generally holding the concept, saying, "I'll be it," and saying "God, send me my first sheep." We need to cross this line, open ourselves to the Spirit and assume the specific gifts.

At The Church of The Saviour we are struggling to follow this Way of openness to the Holy Spirit, through prayer and waiting, and a willingness to accept the specific "manifestation of the Spirit for the common good."* It is our conviction that more and more people will see the light of Christ shining clearly in our lives as we accept these gifts. Our task is to do everything that we can to present the gospel so that people accept Jesus Christ and come to know him, so that they come to be full, committed people. This is what we mean by membership in the Christian church.

* 1 Cor. 12:7, rsv.

IV.
Rejoice
in Your Uniqueness

It is extremely rare to find a person who rejoices in his own uniqueness, who enjoys that bit of God's handiwork which is herself. It is rare because of the heavy price one must pay to arrive at this point and which one must continue to pay. A portion of the cost is expressed in the phrase, "anxiety of separateness." The thought of being separate, alone, and completely responsible is utterly frightening. We surrender our uniqueness rather than bear this anxiety.

To be separate is to know three fundamental things. First, God has addressed us and continues to do so. To know that he addresses "me" is to know that he has spoken to me or to you, calling you by your own unique name. It is to know that our response determines our destiny. It is to be "alone with God."

Second, you come to know "what you are." To put it another way, the way in which you love your neighbor is different from the way anyone else ever loves him. This difference is exactly what is needed—not a sameness. This is also true in the way we love God; we each have a different way, and God needs and wants our unique gift to him.

Third, we know that this strange entity which is "I" is of

indescribable worth even in this moment. God himself has brought me into being—he has expended himself on me, he has acted on my behalf in his Son, Jesus Christ. As faith is exercised and the risk taken of fuller life, a being of incredible beauty emerges. This is the potential of my own being, the outcome of the relationship given me through God's grace in Jesus Christ. He is gathering jewels for his eternal crown and I am one of the jewels.

All of these are fantastic things to believe. They are so fantastic that most of us simply don't believe them. They are part of our religious heritage; we listen with tongue in cheek, sometimes wishing they were true. Of course, they can't be believed apart from an encounter with the living Christ. When this happens, suddenly we can believe what before we could not. We are to love ourselves, simply because God loves us, he delights in us, he takes great joy in us. We are to face the fact that we are different from every other person, and we are to welcome the difference. It is only as the difference is known and actualized that we can be to another that which he needs from us and which we are called to be to him. Only in this way can we be truly an individual, and not just the extension of another. But all of this tends to produce great anxiety, and makes us feel very lonely, at first.

We try to reduce this anxiety in several ways. One is to let God become for us a cosmic father image who needs to be obeyed. If we obey him and if we are good, then he will look after us and protect us. Sometimes we make him a stern father and sometimes a benevolent one, but usually it is a comfort to have him there. Somehow he will see to it that things all come out in the end.

In this view, God is responsible for the real problems of our time. He is responsible because he made it that way. We use this thesis of God to protect ourselves from the living God, and in the name of religion we remain children, permanently.

This God will have to go; we would be better off without him. We are to grow up and we are to take responsibility for the world, rather than using God as a scapegoat. As long as God is merely an authority figure, we shall be stunted—we shall never mature. When things go wrong, we can always blame God.

It's hard to be alone and it's hard to be confronted with a choice and not know until eternity whether it was right. It's hard to live not knowing answers to most of life's basic questions—to live knowing that we may be wrong. We want some form of law and a father God who personifies the security of that law.

But this type of obedience to this type of God will never bring peace and the joy of deep communion. These come from a free, living God and free creatures giving and receiving from one another.

The second thing we do is to try to be like another person. That person appears to us free, fulfilled, adequate, seemingly at peace with himself. We admire him; we look up to her. If we can learn to come at life as he comes at it, then things will go well with us too. If we can respond as she responds, our lives will be improved. We make the person our standard and thus our burden, rather than our life-giving friend. The plain truth is that in many ways we are quite different from the persons we seek to emulate. In many ways we really don't function as they do. We are not to be like them and they are not to be like us. We are to revel in the mystery of the uniqueness they offer to us, and in our own uniqueness. We are to offer ourselves, who are very different from them. This is what the friend needs—not something which is like himself or herself, but that which is over against them, and thus freely offered. This is life-giving.

There are those who try to be like Jesus, who is the most adequate of all friends. There is just enough in the Scriptures to give some support to this position. Paul says "Be imitators

of God." "Brethren, join in imitating me." And we are told
that Christ is the example.* These passages are in the Scripture, but there are more passages which seem to express another point of view. They command us to work out our own
salvation with fear and trembling, for God is at work within
us to will and to work for his good pleasure. Again, it is
"Christ in you, the hope of glory."‡ The "example" is simply
that we see in Jesus Christ the one who is the true man, the
genuine man, the man for others, and what it means to be
fully human. There are others who have entered into the
family likeness of Jesus Christ. We need to know them, to
see them, and such people are guides. But we are never to
imitate them in the sense of becoming a copy of another
person, not even Christ. We are to abide in Christ. We are
to believe, to receive, and to let him take up his abode in us
and bring to fullness our own unique being. It does not involve copying a perfect standard, which, though terribly difficult, is relatively safe.

What's really involved in being a Christian is far more
difficult and exciting and frightening. It is to let Jesus Christ
actually be within us and resuscitate within us all those wild
hopes the world has taught us to distrust. It is the willingness
to live without the security of the law, to live daringly without demanding answers, without having to know right and
wrong. It is a matter of knowing that no matter what mis-
takes I make as I seek to maintain my relationship with him,
there will always be another chance. It is to let him revive
those great expectations that quietly disappeared when I
learned to be "realistic" about my limitations. It is to let the
very word of God in Jesus Christ call to life the dead within
me. It is to let him call me into being.

A third way we seek to reduce the anxiety of separateness is
by holding onto the comfort of always conceiving ourselves as

* Eph. 5:1, rsv; Phil. 3:17, rsv; 1 Pet. 2:21.
‡ Phil. 2:12–13; Col. 1:27, kjv.

a part of some social complex ours by right, and not by grace of God imparted moment by moment to us. The family tempts us most severely at this point. We tend to cling to these relationships and can't imagine being apart from them. We almost demand their perpetuation in the form we know them. Hence our inability to free those closest to us, because we do not know ourselves alone before God. We are unable to rejoice in our own uniqueness and the eternal destiny within the Body of Christ irrespective of the flux of circumstances.

Now it seems almost cruel to tear away these possibilities of reducing the anxiety of separateness. It does something to you to take away the idea of God as the cosmic father. It gives us such a sense of security, and makes it all right for us to be permanently children. The world's starving people are really God's responsibility, as is the housing situation in Washington. Leave it to him. We will carry on our obedience in a very narrow, circumscribed realm. We'll carry on our devotional life, our practices of worship, and be comfortable, while the responsibility for the world is God's. It's comfortable to have people we can admire and emulate—it's always good to have a Christlike example, and we will try hard to be like him. We will surround ourselves with people who are really extensions of ourselves and who are safer because they are around us. We are unwilling and unable to be alone, just alone, before God.

It is only as we give up the safety of seeing ourselves part of some social complex that we can in freedom belong to those that God is giving us at the moment. It is only in separateness that there can be genuine communion and a lessening of the anxiety and the knowing of the presence and peace of God.

PART THREE

THE INTERN MEMBER
OF A MISSION GROUP

V.
The Intern Member's Commitment

Introduction

A covenant entered into when one is inwardly ready can greatly further one's growth.

A covenant entered into legalistically, because of the requirements of the group, when there is not an internal readiness, will be disastrous to the person as well as to the group.

The terms of the covenant must be not only clearly understood but desired at the deepest level. Different periods of preparation are necessary for different people.

Accountability—so vital to a group's health, is only growth-producing when the covenant has been freely embraced and deeply desired.

Intern Member's Commitment

I commit myself to the covenant of my mission group. By this I declare my willingness to be held accountable for the disciplines that the members have made explicit. I recognize that in making this pledge I am committing myself to involvement with people who are not like me—whose opinions and ways may be in opposition to my own. I thus declare my willingness to be stretched in uncomfortable ways, and to live in the tension and pain of unresolved relationships until differences shall be transcended and hurt transmuted.

I acknowledge that the cornerstone of this community is Jesus Christ, Servant and Liberator—the One who said, "Love one another, as I have loved you. There is no greater love than this, that a man should lay down his life for his friends" (John 15:12–13, NEB). In committing myself to the covenant of the mission I confess my willingness to take upon myself the life style of servant. I will endeavor to grow in my availability to each person in the group and I will join in the struggle for the liberation of the oppressed.

I will seek not only to receive, but to give; not only to be loved, but to love. I will give myself to discovering what it means to be a free person in community and what it means to be a community of free persons.

I recognize that though I am bound by the covenant of my mission group, I am ever free to break with it—never by default, but by open decision arrived at through meditation and in conversation with members of my group.

I celebrate this day because I believe that in binding myself in this covenant, I will be given new possibilities for a life of growth, freedom and devotion.

Notes

1. The purpose of the category of intern membership is to enable a searching person to explore more deeply what it means to be a part of a servant people and to discover whether he or she can say yes to membership as experienced by The Church of The Saviour community.

2. An intern member is asked to complete the basic courses in the School of Christian Living unless substitute experiences are approved by group members. It is important to know that those who have tried to carry the intern member's responsibility and simultaneously to take classes in the school have found it extremely difficult. For this reason it is advised that an applicant for intern membership complete at least two classes in the school before joining a mission group.

3. Because an intern member is endeavoring to live his or her way into a deeper and fuller belonging to this expression of the church, he or she lives by the disciplines of the members with one exception: The intern member gives proportionately of his gross income beginning at 5 percent. (A pledge card is completed.)

4. Intern members are those who feel that they can best realize their own potentials through being bound with others in a covenant that includes corporate disciplines for deepening the life of devotion and the life of involvement in the world's need.

5. Anyone making application should be fully acquainted with the disciplines and committed to them before assuming intern status. This can be accomplished best by conferences with the spiritual director and the moderator of the group. If, after the conference, an applicant feels good about proceeding, the moderator and spiritual director will seek the confirmation of the group. The group will then seek the confirmation of the council.

6. Intern members are always free to leave the group, but

it is important to make this decision in conversation with group members. If an intern reaches the conclusion that membership in The Church of The Saviour is a direction in which he or she does not want to move, then he or she has the responsibility of withdrawing from the group, but it is again an action taken only after being in conversation with one's mission community.

VI.
The Sponsor's
Guide

Introduction

The head of the church is Jesus Christ, the Son of God. It is Christ himself who calls each person into membership in his Body; joining is not by human invitation. Each of us needs to be sure that the call we have is unmistakably Christ's, and to understand thoroughly the implications of belonging to this body; otherwise the pressures in such a closely knit fellowship can be intolerable.

Those who wish to join our fellowship should have a clear understanding of the particular calling of The Church of The Saviour. Total commitment to Christ and disciplined lives are not for the purpose of earning one's way to heaven. Rather, they are for the glory of God to release the power of the Holy Spirit in our corporate witness. This cannot take place amid a people undisciplined to the bidding of Christ.

To each person who expresses a desire to become a member of The Church of The Saviour, we assign a sponsor. The sponsor's task is to help the applicant examine his or her call, as well as to discuss with him something of what is involved in the membership commitment. It is important for the applicant to have the opportunity of examining his or her motivations for joining with another person. (Am I hoping to gain status? To gain a feeling of "belonging"? To be able to command more steady nurture? To have a sense of achievement?) Such motives are sometimes unconscious, but misunderstood they will hinder a member's ability to live creatively within the body.

Another area to examine is the applicant's already existing relationship within the fellowship of the committed. If he or she has not become acquainted with a large percentage of the members, there is doubt that he knows what he is undertaking in wanting to be part of this particular unit of Christ's Body. If he has not already sought out and made opportunity for conversations or actual visits with the individual members, the sponsor may take the initiative in arranging for him to do so with as many of the members as possible.

Candidates will be interested in knowing about the other mission groups in the church, what they are doing, who is in them, what their purposes are. They will make it their business to find out about them through talking to other members or by reading their newsletters, and joining in prayer for them. There should be a solidarity with other members, even though paths do not necessarily cross in mission; this solidarity is necessary when one participates in decisions affecting the whole congregation. Mission groups, in a sense, "back each other up."

The actual steps taken before one makes a public commitment are the following:

1. Classes in the School of Christian Living. All members of The Church of The Saviour have completed courses in Old Testament, New Testament, Christian Ethics, Christian Growth, and Christian Doctrine, although only two of these are prerequisite to joining a mission group as an intern.

2. Sponsorship. The candidate's mission group as a whole may work through the sponsor's guide with the applicant or

may appoint a member to do it. The sponsoring member stays
in close communication with the applicant's mission group.

The sponsor will cover, in whatever way he thinks appropriate, four major areas during his meeting with the applicant:

(1) The importance of total commitment to Christ

(2) The meaning of "Church" and of "Community"

(3) The meaning of "Mission" and "Ecumenicity"

(4) Specific responsibilities of a member of The Church of
The Saviour.

3. Required Reading. During sponsorship the candidate
should read (if he hasn't already) Call to Commitment and
Journey Inward, Journey Outward by Elizabeth O'Connor.*

4. Spiritual Autobiography. Each candidate writes a spiritual
autobiography which acquaints the other members with his
or her background in the life of the spirit, previous church
orientation, the high points in his or her life as they have
affected spiritual growth, and where he or she is in relationship to Christ. The autobiography is first shared with members of the mission group. When the sponsor or sponsors
agree that the candidate is ready to join, he or she meets with
the church council and reads the paper. On the affirmation
of the council, the candidate is accepted into full membership and a date is set for making the final commitment at
a Sunday worship before the congregation.

5. Chapel Vigil. During the week before making the final
commitment, the prospective member spends an hour in the
chapel in a vigil of prayer, and then signs the commitment
book.

6. Formal Commitment. The following Sunday the candidate, surrounded by the members of his or her mission group,
stands before the congregation and makes his or her commitment.‡

---

* Call to Commitment (New York: Harper & Row, 1963). Journey Inward, Journey Outward (New York: Harper & Row, 1968).

‡ The commitment is given on page 140.

The Sponsor's Guide

THE IMPORTANCE OF COMMITMENT TO JESUS CHRIST

We believe that commitment to Christ is the means whereby we are enabled to make God's kingship real in our lives, as this way is described in the Sermon on the Mount. The gospel makes two things clear: God's unlimited love and forgiveness (grace) in his gift of Christ as our deliverer and Lord; and God's unlimited demand upon us to relate to others with this same love and forgiveness which we ourselves have received.

Partial allegiance results in blockage of the channels through which God's enabling power flows into our lives; therefore, we believe that Christ must have priority in everything. To join this church is to yield one's life unreservedly to him. This is a present act, but it is also a future resolve, for as we grow we become aware of the many areas in our lives that have not yet been brought under his mastery. We believe that the only way to arrive at total commitment is through the school of discipline which we ourselves elect as a means of developing and deepening our spiritual capacities. We must ask ourselves these questions:

a. What has been my experience of God's grace in my life? In what ways have I experienced God's love, power, and forgiveness?

b. What correlations are there between how God has related to me in Christ and how I see myself relating to others? Wherein has Christ made a difference in who I am and how I relate? Where do I see discrepancies between who I am and how I relate, and what I feel Christ calls me to be?

c. At what point would I say that Christ has less than full priority in my life? What are some of the means by which I could move toward deeper commitment?

112

THE MEANING OF "CHURCH" AND OF "COMMUNITY"

The Church is the fellowship of those who belong to one another in Christ. It is the family of God, bound to him through Christ, and bound to one another because of devotion to him. It is the Body of Christ. It is the community of the forgiven, of the justified. The Church, although it exists as an end in itself, also exists to lose its life for the redemption of mankind.

It is the peculiar calling of The Church of The Saviour to be a disciplined group working toward total commitment to Christ. Out of this calling comes its emphasis on prayer, on ecumenicity, and all its other distinctive features. The spirit of the church provides an atmosphere of fellowship and a sphere of service for Christians of varying doctrinal positions and interpretations within the stream of historic and evangelical Christianity.

Although each of us must stand alone before God, no one of us can be a Christian by ourselves. In joining the "Church" one becomes a part of the Body of Christ. A part which is not united with other parts is useless. My church is that group of people with whom I am in close spiritual association; if I am not living in such association, I have no church no matter what "congregation" I may belong to. The church is the *laos*, the people of God, and the people of God always live in community. It is in this community that my gifts are evoked and it is here that I help evoke the gifts of others. The church is the seedbed and the garden in which the fruits of the Spirit grow.

Such growth will take place only if there has been a definite call, not only to live in community, but also to maintain the disciplined life; otherwise, the discipline of the community will not be tolerable. (By discipline we mean training in the use of our capacities, our time, and our resources; discipline is never an end in itself or a way of earning salvation.)

This unit in Christ's Body is one which professes a systematic openness to grace. Membership is not for just anyone who wants to be saved. Discipline will always be part of our life together. It is agreed that the stakes are high; discipline is the price of power and effectiveness in our individual and corporate witness. There must be freedom in this area, however, and the purpose of an ordered way needs to be well understood. We must always be aware of the danger of settling for legalistic forms, for, insofar as the disciplines are practiced merely legalistically and perfunctorily, we will indeed speak with a hollow sound.

To become a member of the community of The Church of The Saviour is to be a member of one of the mission groups. One may change mission groups, or bring into being a new group if none exists in an area where one feels called to work, but to be a member means to participate fully in a mission group, subject to its covenant. One remains free to break the covenant should it become an alien pressure rather than an imperative from within, but this should never be by default. In such an eventuality, the member is asked to discuss his or her situation with the council or with members of the mission group before making the final decision to withdraw from the covenant. An arm or a leg cannot break off without the body's recognizing its loss; equally we feel that a person who finds it necessary to leave this community represents a loss to the total body. We would want to understand the reasons for anyone's leaving—especially insofar as they might represent failure on our part to be the church for them —and we would want to make their departure an occasion for solemn acknowledgment and mourning, as well as a time in which we can joyfully release them to whatever new directions their life may be taking.

Dropping out of membership, however, does not necessarily mean dropping out of the church's life. Many other groups in the church may meet the needs of the person: informal discussion groups, prayer groups, counseling groups, classes in the School of Christian Living. Members have been known to drop out of membership for several years, to rejoin when they are able to resume the responsibilities and life style of membership.

In the light of what the church is and our call to community, we need to ask ourselves questions like the following:

a. Am I willing to be joined with members of this community so that this context of relationships becomes the primary place where my life is identified, rooted, and lived out?

b. Am I willing to be joined to each member of the congregation for better or for worse, realizing that Christ is the one who has called us together and given us to each other?

c. "Walk . . . with all lowliness and meekness, with long-suffering, forbearing one another in love."* Am I willing to let my brother or my sister be a burden? Will I bear with a brother in the abuse of my freedom, preserving fellowship with him through forgiveness? Will I bear with my sister when my sister's freedom collides with my autonomy? In times of misunderstanding, hurt, and alienation, will I seek out my brother or my sister and endeavor to become reconciled to them?

d. What spiritual gifts do I feel have been given to me? Which of these do I feel have been relatively well developed, and to what extent are they contributing to the upbuilding of the community? How do we help evoke gifts in others?

e. The commitment of The Church of The Saviour is made specific in disciplines that form the covenant the members make with one another. Do I see these disciplines as essential to my growth? Am I willing to assume the obligation of holding others accountable for these disciplines, and am I

* Eph. 4:1–2, KJV.

willing to open myself to the obligations that others must assume for me?

THE MEANING OF "MISSION" AND OF "ECUMENICITY"

The Christian community is bound on a twofold journey—one inward, the other outward. The inward journey is to find Christ within oneself and within others, and through him to come into the presence of God. The outward journey is to find Christ and to be with him as he is at work in the world. This is mission—to be with Christ, bringing into being the kingdom of God in the world. Thus the church is mission. As Brunner says, a fire is burning—no burning, no fire. So with the church—no mission, no church.

Each member and prospective member should know something of and be in touch with the separate group missions of The Church of The Saviour and should be led to understand how they all together constitute the one united total mission of the community. The group mission never exists solitarily; it is an integral part of the whole that is the church. Every member should read at least one book on the Ecumenical Movement to deepen his or her belonging to the total Body of Christ in its varied expressions throughout the world. In joining The Church of The Saviour, one should have a sense of joining the worldwide Church.

It should be a measure of one's maturity that one knows oneself as a member of the Christian church wherever it exists, in sickness or in health. The candidate should be helped to realize that all churches together are the Body of Christ. If the Body is really being crucified elsewhere, our reaction must be that this is an occasion for love and healing rather than for judgment or resentment.

As members we need to examine our commitment to mission and to ecumenicity:

a. Do I feel that the inward and outward journeys are in

balance for me? If not, am I willing to do what I can to make them more so?

b. The Church of The Saviour makes concrete its belonging to other churches in the allocations it makes in its budget, in its distribution of literature, in its ministry to visitors and in its interpretation of the church's life to those who are exploring the faith through the missions and School of Christian Living. Does this have meaning for me?

c. As the full congregation of members has the responsibility of making concrete its belonging to the whole of Christendom, each individual mission group must make real its belonging to other mission groups. This may simply mean supporting another group by one's presence at a called meeting, praying for it, interpreting its life for strangers or giving it financial assistance or aid in crisis. If I feel out of touch with a group or at variance with it, what is my responsibility?

d. What is my feeling about the church in which I grew up? About my responsibilities toward other churches in general?

e. Am I aware that when I drop out of my mission group I am dropping out of membership in the church?

THE OBLIGATIONS OF MEMBERSHIP

Before making a final commitment, every member agrees to assume the obligations of membership and to take his or her part in the various aspects of the church's structure.

1. *Annual recommitment.* Each year members review the basic loyalties, insights, dreams, and principles of the church, and engage in self-searching, to be sure their ideas and loyalties are still in harmony with the calling of this particular congregation.

2. Each member carries some important function or responsibility in his or her group, and thus in the church. There are no passengers; all are crew members.

3. Sooner or later, all members serve a term on the church council. These are elected from their own mission groups, and rotation takes place every six months so all the council is not new at one time. If a member must be absent, he or she is responsible for letting the church office know so it can be reported at the meeting. The size and business nature of such meetings mean that they require work and the often painful process of long deliberation. All basic decisions of the church are made at the council meetings, and should represent consensus of the full membership.

However, individual council members are not there merely to reflect the consensus of their respective groups. They have been chosen by the group and sent forth as free agents to use their own God-directed judgment in helping to make policy.

4. The *financing* of the church depends upon members' tithing as a minimum. Members may begin with a tithe but should progress to proportionate giving of their income. Giving is an outgrowth of Christian commitment; the church is opposed to dissipating its energies from the central spiritual tasks at hand by trying to raise money through bazaars, dinners, and the like.

THE MARKS OF BELONGING

When all is said and done, formal membership is merely a public recognition of a belonging that is already in effect. What are the marks of belonging? They are love, joy, forgiveness, and dependence on God rather than on people.*

Concerning love: "That we are commanded to love, and cannot, is our dilemma and our despair" (Florence Allshorn). Do I face the fact that I am unable to love? Am I consciously pursuing some plan of Christian growth that enables me "to

---

* It is suggested that the candidate meditate on this section during the hour spent in the chapel in the week preceding the making of the public commitment.

comprehend with all the saints what is the breadth and length and height and depth, and to know the love of Christ which surpasses knowledge," that I "may be filled with all the fullness of God"?* Am I open to new truth in this area—scientific, theological, psychological?

Concerning joy: Do I recognize the fact that joy is the mark of the Christ? And if I do not have that joy (not just happiness or pleasure), am I coming to grips with whatever there is in my life that is shutting me off from that joy?

Concerning forgiveness: Are my standards for those in the membership so high that when I am offended by them (for instance, by a careless word or by apparent slight or neglect) I allow my faith in them to waver or to be destroyed? How well do I grasp the fact that the church knows itself to be a community of sinners whose life together is based on each one's knowing himself or herself to be forgiven by God and therefore being bound to forgive one's brother or sister?

Concerning dependence on God rather than on people: Am I secure enough in my relationship with Christ so that I am no longer threatened when confronted by someone who is uncongenial? Am I firm in my conviction that our fellowship, the fellowship of the Holy Spirit, is based on Christ's love for us, our love for him, and our *agape* love for one another?

* Eph. 3:18–19, rsv.

VII.
Spiritual
Autobiographies

Introduction

The final stage of sponsorship into the membership of The Church of The Saviour is the writing of what we call a "spiritual autobiography." By sharing this biography with the mission group first, then with the church council, interns come into full membership—for the autobiography is an account of spiritual pilgrimage which has brought them to this time of commitment.

Several examples from these varied accounts are included for those who wish to become familiar with this kind of sharing of histories which has deepened immeasurably our knowing one another.

Autobiography of Sharon McCririe

There are early memories of sitting in church with my mother, sucking Lifesavers and scribbling on the bulletin, and every Sunday responding as best I could to the altar call in the Baptist church but not being sure anything happened.

When I was eight, I sensed Christ's presence and his love for me in a way that was more real, and I responded by telling him to come into my heart—I wanted to be his. I'll never forget coming out of the church and being absolutely caught up in the blueness of the sky and the green green of the weeds that had managed to escape the city sprayer growing around palm trees in little circles of dirt left in the sidewalk.

My spiritual upbringing was with a mother who really did know and love the Lord and a father who embodied his faith. In our fundamentalist Bible church I grew up with an emphasis on the divinity of Christ, his saviorhood and his lordship. "Right doctrine," which included our perfection in Christ, was held in greatest importance. The result was a vivid awareness of the nearness of God, belief in the Scriptures as reliable communiqués from God, experiences of living in response to God's direction, and a compelling concern that others be open to the creative life of Christ.

With these positive inputs there was a complement of negatives: a judgmental attitude toward those outside the fold and a concern for the salvation of the soul as separate from society. But the most detrimental force the church exerted on me was to squelch all inclinations and actions not perfect in Christ and based in right doctrine as these were understood by the group. I couldn't be a sinner or a seeker without being labeled "out of fellowship," which amounted to ostracism. The result for me was so to concentrate on my perfection in Christ that I became separated from my sin—a phenomenon which God is still rectifying.

After getting my secondary teaching credentials, I married Jack. Three years later we joined the Peace Corps and went to teach in Malaysia—an experience which contributed its bit to the sifting and refining process in my life. We heard comments when we came home on how much we had sacrificed, but the sacrifice would have been to stay where everything was familiar and where I thought I knew what was going on. Because then I might never have learned how little I was aware of. I might never have come up against the limiting and detrimental nature of my preconceived notions or recognized the destructiveness of my rigidity. I might never have recognized how dependent on my surroundings I am for inner peace or how strong my past is in shaping my present reactions. I might have missed my need for constant breaking and reshaping to be enabled to receive new inputs. I might have missed the truth that what is different can be right too, and what is new can be better than what I have known to be best. I might never have realized how unique and full of surprises every person is or how new every familiar thing is. I might have missed really needing God to survive. I might have missed being caught in his love and being really happy independent of circumstances and close to people different from myself.

I had read *Call to Commitment* before going to Malaysia, and I sensed then that The Church of The Saviour was the first Christian community I knew of where I felt I could put my full weight down. We immediately found the church on our return to the States, and I enrolled in a New Testament course. Living into Mark 16 opened up the next year for me. The angel's word to the Marys after the Resurrection was "He will go on before you into Galilee and you will see him there."* My response was "I know you've come before but

* Mark 16:7.

just where is the Galilee where I will see you?" And the response came, "17th and R." (We lived at that corner.)

A few days later I met Doris. She had a well-developed knack for making self-destructive decisions. I first saw her lying drunk and half-dressed between dirty sheets, covered with boils, and I knew I had found Galilee. When she began to suspect she mattered to me, the testing began and the trying to hurt to make sure of her position. Our relationship intruded throughout my days at unexpected times, and I wished I could just walk away. But at the same time I knew there could be no freeing in running. Deep within I felt she was given to me and I to her.

I felt pain with her and her children in her situation, but much of the pain was my own inner grappling, a struggle with my own motives, my own selfishness, my own impatience and fallibility and powerlessness to enable her to get on her feet. Ego-involvement with her making it was no small factor. Wanting to be liked jumped up and shouted when I sensed that a hard line needed to be taken that might cause her to turn against me. And I entered further into the creation of my own life to which suffering gave impetus.

Now she and some of her neighbors are among the most significant people in my life, and I suspect that if there had been no friction and no mutual rubbing I would have missed them and would have missed a significant shaping of my own being. Some of the principal gifts given were the habit of prayer in relationships, a faith that others belong to the Lord, that he is the source of growth and the director of our lives together, and a staying power when relationships are at sword's edge. All of these I've been grateful for, especially since there was to be so much darkness in the days ahead.

Another special time with the Lord came when we were in India two years later. I dreamed of Mary Cosby saying "Memorize Psalm 52." A few days later a large diesel compressor came loose from its tow cable and hit the car I was traveling in head on, pinning me between the dash and the seat. My hip had to be relocated. As I came out from under the ether I thought I was in heaven because I was absolutely surrounded and infused with love and I heard a voice say, "The other boys are all right. Jahangir (the driver) is all right. Jack and Shanti (my daughter) will be all right. Your hip will be all right." Whatever happened then lingered, and for six weeks my life was joy, prayer, creativity, peace, awareness of God's Spirit, and sheer love in entering into it with those who came to my hospital room.

The first thing I asked for in the hospital was a Bible. The first part of Psalm 52 was not to have any meaning till later, but the last two verses stood out as the message for the event: "But I am like a green olive tree in the house of God: I trust in the mercy of God for ever and ever. I will praise thee for ever, because thou hast done it: and I will wait on thy name; for it is good before thy saints."*

I flinch as I have flashes of the impact and remember the feeling of being torn apart by the traction, and the itching of the scabs the beetles left all over my face, and the episodes with the bedpan, where privacy about such matters is of no value. But overall, I was surrounded in warmth and gratitude. The collision turned out to be no accident, but a gift.

A few months later Jack told me he was considering divorce. It was then that I really came up against my own helplessness and frailty. There was nothing I could do. I was faced with my own self-righteous destructiveness and need for redemption. It was then that my dark selves began to emerge—darker and more operative than I had even imagined. I had to get acquainted with them and get a handle on my own actions, reactions and old-time feelings. I felt like a bomb had burst inside and I was on the garbage heap—at the point of either

* Ps. 52:8–9.

being recycled or becoming a pollutant. I refused the latter—
probably out of the same stubbornness that had made me
such an insensitive wife. Then began a whole new dialogue
with the Lord and between my selves, and the beginning of
new dialogue with Jack.

At this time my dreams became some of my most valuable
allies, putting me in touch with resident evil and conflicting
desires. One night I dreamed I was being bitten by large
vipers which I was able to shake off. In the next scene I was
selling small vipers and lining them up so they could slither
off into a crowded road to do their damage. The more specific
vipers I recognized, the more I recognized their strength, and
the more aware I became that I could do nothing to break
their tyranny.

An inner seesawing was going on. On the one hand I longed
to repent and be crucified with Christ and really be made
nothing so I could be God's. But on the other, I was putting
every effort into trying to wriggle away from the nails. I
couldn't die. I couldn't even lie down and let the job be done.
The truth of verse 5 of Psalm 52 became my hope: "God
shall likewise destroy thee for ever, he shall take thee away,
and pluck thee out of the land of thy dwelling place, and root
thee out of the land of the living."

So God would do the rooting out! What a relief to be able
to relax a bit and pass the buck to him. Surely now I could
enter into the stillness. Surely now I could just enjoy being
with the Lord. Expectantly I continued the inward pilgrimage
—only to find in worship a seeking of gifts and glory, in the
midst of silence meandering thoughts, and in the midst of
praise, backslapping for how well I was doing.

And still, the Lord keeps forgiving me. He keeps breaking
a little more tyranny to give me a little more working room.
This experience of his forgiveness has resulted in a kind of
freedom to move within, and more acceptance (still mingled
with impatience) of what I find. Something about being able

to name my vipers has robbed them of their power. And there's a freedom coming with other people—just plain enjoyment of their being—a desire to know and be known. The more at home I am with myself, the more at home I am with others.

Jack and I have separated. The past seven months have been full of pain, but also of growth and joy and awareness of God's love and power. It's strange how it can be so bad and also so very good. As I have drawn near to Christ, he has drawn near to me and has given me the gift of my own unlived pain. With him I've been able to experience my clutching of my own life, and my possessiveness. I've felt the pain it wreaks in my own body and its destructiveness. As I've gotten to the point of being able to clutch no more, I've been enabled to relax and receive whatever is given. I've been enabled to sob and be lonely and be angry at some of the crumby deals I've been dealt, and God has been there in the pain. He's changing me. The experience of the pain instead of decreasing has increased, but in it and through the community I'm finding great love and support.

It has taken blows for me to get the picture that I have a right to nothing and that being in God is everything. It has been in the gift of suffering that I have most experienced God's presence, and primarily through suffering that my experience of the unencumbered life has grown. It is here that my grasping of my own life has been weakened, and tiny windows have been opened into the contemplative life. They leave me glimpsing how very far I have to go, but most grateful for my Lord and for who I am becoming.

Autobiography of Bud Thar

I was born the third of five children at 6 A.M., October 26, 1940 in Paw Paw, Michigan. I still love early morning—God's gift to me. "Morning has gold in its mouth." We lived at Agreeable Acres—our fruit farm. For eight winters we went to Fort Myers, Florida, for several months while my father managed a food packing house.

I come from a family Roman Catholic on my father's side and Lutheran on my mother's. When we moved to Agreeable Acres the Methodist church was nearest; in Florida we attended a Baptist church.

At two I had a near-fatal hernia and I have appreciated life as gift since then, feeling God has a reason for keeping me here. That summer my dad carried me around the farm in a bushel basket and we developed a bond that exists today—a special bond that helps both of us. Also my father helped me understand God through his character, rather than hindering my faith and growth. I mean the concept I had of man's and God's power complementing each other. My mother is a pillar of faith in a very pragmatic way, and a vital and giving person.

Becoming a child in the Christian faith started for me in real ways after a 4-H camp vesper service when the simple question was asked, "What are the first four words in the Bible?" (I was nine at the time.) I didn't know, and my ignorance humbled me, and I started to read the Bible. I had attended Sunday school and Bible school (I remember being spanked to make me go when I was five), and vowed that when I grew up I'd never go to church.

When I was twelve I took membership classes and joined the Methodist church. I was questioning, and often stayed into late hours at my minister's office talking. He let me take an active role in assisting in the worship, at weddings, and at other times. Rev. John Wesley Smith was influential—he always said I could do much in the ministry. He was in seminary (1956–58) while serving our church. He gave me more responsibility than my family would allow me on the farm, so I responded and grew. When I was a junior in high school I sort of planned to head toward pre-theology, though I did very well in science during the U.S. "sputnik" push to advance. When I enrolled at Michigan State my adviser, a natural scientist, said "Why don't you become an engineer and pay three preachers?"

I was active in the Wesley Foundation and especially was attracted to the early Wednesday morning communions. After my freshman year I was selected to help represent the U.S. in India. Here I found God's concern for the individual among the masses. I met world leaders. The scope of my call broadened.

I was president of eight organizations and a member of thirteen of them at once—church, school, national. I counseled kids at a YMCA camp, fell in love, traveled, worked in the migrant ministry, looked at seminaries, and chose Boston over Union, Yale, Northwestern and Duke, as well as Wesley. I was youth director for Central Methodist Church in Lansing, a delegate to Israel for six months (where I met my favorite philosopher, Martin Buber) and led twenty teenagers on "Operation Friendship" to Costa Rica for a month of Peace Corps type work.

During my college years I went home to be with my father (at the time he was severely depressed) and mother and manage the farm. Those were difficult days, but my faith and trust in God grew, for I came to feel that God is on either side of suicide. My grandfather, a farmer, was always financially successful, and he undermined my father who was the buffer for us from his very authoritarian German father who believed in breaking people—always critical, never affirming. My father, the only son, was disinherited, which carried the bad relationship beyond the grave.

In India, my diary records a day in hell. I was the youngest of the Americans, and our group, undergoing some adjustment and cultural shock, projected its problems on me. I learned what hell must be like and how terrible it is to be out of relationship. Though this was with people, I'm sure it must be that bad or worse when one turns one's back on God.

In the summer of 1964, before seminary, I visited The Potter's House while I worked at the 4-H Center in Washington. I played chess, later I came to the morning worship, and eventually came to The Church of The Saviour. I heard a lot about the retreat center at Dayspring—fellow seminarians had had great experiences there.

My early days in seminary were forty days in the wilderness. The black kids of Roxbury kept me interested, and work in the ghetto and in Selma with Dr. King—these were very moving spiritually for me. In Boston I often went over to Cambridge to the Quaker meeting house. I enjoyed the Quaker encounter with God, with no intermediary, but a direct listening and confrontation. No one to blame about the sermon, setting, etc. Just me, the individual, and God through Christ.

I could not respond to the call of ordination; I didn't feel called to the pulpit or to the church as an institution. My advisor was the one who translated the poet Tagore into English. I think I am somewhat Jewish in theology—who are we to tell God what he is like?—and a mystic in faith, feeling that God through Christ speaks to the individual. I don't feel that Christianity has a monopoly on God and Christ. The Logos is too big and powerful for most organizations to contend with. What happens when one institutionalizes love? The home should be a temple—as Friday evening in the Hebrew home.

After 1965 in Boston and seminary, I looked for international responsibilities, and I received a grant to the Seminar on Congress and Foreign Policy sponsored by Quakers in Washington. We interviewed Senators and Representatives about conversion of the military budget, recognition of China. A project of mine was the funding of international education. I soon discovered that the Pentagon had most of the marbles and spent them training people around the world to use slingshots—in a time of much deeper needs. That was the summer of the Gulf of Tonkin fiasco.

I enjoy meditation, and say a prayer in all parts of my day —before a date for example, to acknowledge God's presence. Communion is special for me. I doubt if Siri and I would be married were it not for a milk and bread communion in the Agreeable Acres kitchen three months before our wedding. Forgiveness, reconciliation, love, peace, hope, faith.

Later there was my marriage to Siri and the birth of our two children. The co-creative relationship with God was felt through the gift of the children. I knew light, warmth, and the joy of the welding experience of marriage—they became real in the delivery room in those precious moments after both Jonathan and Christine were born.

Call and vision for me have been international relations, cross-cultural conflict and understanding, as well as domestic justice. Each step in my work in the rural life of the nation— migrants and abroad—has been balanced by another domestic ghetto experience that has again led to international opportunities.

In the summer of 1971, as our family drove through Czechoslovakia, I learned anew that freedom isn't free. Political structures everywhere oppress people and servant leadership is rare. This has led me to the Dunamis mission group. In Dunamis I have the opportunity to pray for persons in political power and to allow God to use me as a pastor-prophet by speaking the truth in love.

April 1971

Autobiography of David Dorsey

My formal ties with the organized church began when I became a member of the Cradle Roll of the First Baptist Church of Oak Park, Illinois, at the age of three. As I look back on it, I believe this was my only church relationship where I did not spend a great deal of time questioning and examining the theology and activities of the group to which I belonged.

I was the oldest of four children—David, Diane, Daryl, and Daniel. Friends would send Christmas cards addressed to "Mr. and Mrs. Dorsey and the 4 D's." My parents encouraged all of us to be independent and resourceful. Praise was given for accomplishment, and accomplishment often became the sole objective of my efforts. I still struggle with the feeling that my self-worth is totally dependent on what I produce rather than on any intrinsic value.

I grew up in two Methodist churches in the western suburbs of Chicago. During this period—from kindergarten through high school—attending church services and related social events every Sunday was as much an accepted part of my life as brushing my teeth every morning, and required about the same degree of discipline and commitment.

I did a lot of exploring during my years at the University of Michigan. I was active in Methodist and Congregational student groups, attended services at a Disciples' church, took communion regularly at an Episcopal church and took courses in theology and doctrine at the Roman Catholic church and the Hillel Foundation. I also seriously considered entering the ministry at this point, but decided that my gifts were primarily analytic—that I could become a good, socially conscious mathematician or businessman, but would never be more than a mediocre minister. My experience also showed that there seemed to be a definite shortage in the former category, but there was no shortage in the latter.

In my senior year I applied to the Methodist Board of Missions to work as a short-term missionary—aiming at a business manager or teaching position in Africa. However, although I had strong references and passed all other tests with flying colors, on a personality profile I zigged where I should have zagged and was eventually rejected. The Board of Missions felt that I could neither adapt to new situations nor was able to get along with people.

The United States Peace Corps felt differently and I was able to rest, reflect, and read a fair amount of theology during my two years teaching mathematics in Ghana. This experience was followed by two years of intense education in finance and international business at the Harvard Business School. As I look back on it, I think these four years can be characterized by an attitude that said: "All right, God, I gave you a real chance to use me, you didn't want it, so the hell with you. From now on I can do very well on my own, thank you."

In March of 1965, I visited Washington for a week to interview government agencies for a summer job between my two years at the business school. Alan and Mary Carol Dragoo, the couple with whom I stayed, introduced me to The Church of The Saviour. During the following summer I became familiar with and was very much impressed by the people at this church. Not that so many were so brilliant, but that so many were so sick. I saw a group of people, unsuccessful by the world's standards, find three foster homes for Junior Village children one Saturday afternoon. It reminded me of another group of socially and culturally disadvantaged persons led by a dense and cowardly fisherman. It seemed to say that the church of Christ is built more on the rock of commitment than the sands of intelligence and training.

From the summer of 1966 to the summer of 1968 I was very active at The Church of The Saviour. The church was the culmination of the types of church groups to which I had always belonged. It was a very satisfying and meaningful part of my life. It was very comfortable. When my job became boring at the Agency for International Development in 1968, I was offered a position in the corporate office of Allied Chemical in New York City. I looked forward to testing my business and financial abilities on Wall Street and had at the same time decided not to pursue membership in The Church of The Saviour. I believe this was primarily because I felt there was no peer group of single adults with which I could identify. At that time I saw The Church of The Saviour as a vehicle in which I could maintain a comfortable relationship with God and like-thinking persons.

About January 1969, in New York, I became aware that I was becoming progressively more frustrated and less happy. In fact, I could not recall really being happy during any of the past decade. I was a member of a vital church community. I had an impressive bachelor apartment in Greenwich Village. I knew many attractive young women, most of whom I could take out whenever I wanted to any of the cafes or theatres that were within easy walking distance of my apartment. I was active in New York politics and knew on a first-name basis the officers of the most active and influential political club in Manhattan. I was making a lot of money at age thirty, and was impressing everyone who knew me at Allied Chemical.

Using the catalyst of group therapy and later individual therapy, I became more and more aware that I was following rules and standards laid down for me by others. I was achieving according to what others had indicated were measures of success rather than doing what I really wanted to do. This life style was also killing my spiritual life. I saw the necessity of being totally committed to God's will rather than using my sliding scale of "to what extent can I afford to do God's will this week?" I said, "Lord, here am I. What would you have me do?" And the Lord said "It's all very simple. I just want you to let go of everything." So I let go of everything. I quit

my job, broke the lease on my apartment, resigned my political
and church positions, said goodbye to friends, packed all my
earthly goods in one U-Haul trailer and moved back to
Washington.

This was a basic turning point in my life. Previously I had
always planned and set goals with painstaking precision. Two
years before I even applied to Harvard I had sent for an application form so I could acquire the experience to match the
questions that were asked. Now I was letting go of self-
determination entirely. I was determined to go wherever the
Spirit led without asking for insight or guarantees. I remembered the quotation from a church bulletin at The Church of
The Saviour on a first Sunday in January: "And I said to the
man who stood at the gate of the year: 'Give me a light that I
may tread safely into the unknown.' And he said: 'Go out
into the darkness and put your hand into the hand of God.
That shall be to you better than light and safer than a known
way.' "*

I returned to Washington and lived in Bob Gray's attic
while I did some volunteer social work and wrestled with
what kind of job was really God's call. The same problem was
still present. How do I use the gifts of financial analysis and
strategic planning in the context of a full Christian commitment?

In April 1970, after four months of unemployment (my
savings had just about run out), I was offered and accepted
a job in the Commissioner's Office of the Food and Drug
Administration. I was able to initiate programs that I felt
would help protect consumers from unsafe foods and ineffec-
tive drugs. However, government was still government, and
would accept only a limited amount of change. In September
1972 I felt I had done all I could do—the call was no longer
at FDA. I struggled again to find my Christian vocation. I

* "God Knows," Minnie Louise Haskins.

knew it was to be in Washington and would use my administrative background. That was all I did know.

Two great gifts have been given to me over the past two years. One is the integration of my financial and administrative training with my Christian commitment. I am now working as executive director of Wellspring, a mission which seeks to help enable church renewal by sharing the life of The Church of The Saviour with other Christian communities. Rather than looking forward to weekends, I now look forward to the next week of negotiating contracts to build church facilities at Dayspring or further developing our Wellspring Participant Program.

The second gift is The Servant Community. This is a community of committed Christians who live and worship together, share household work and expenses, and explore what the leading of the Holy Spirit is for our lives. There have been many changes in the two brief years of our existence. Our response to call has changed and clarified, people have come and gone, but we have provided a place of growth for ourselves and a place of lodging for persons visiting our larger church community. The Servant Community consists of only five persons at present. But just as in other areas of my life, it will grow and become the witness it is meant to be if I and others called to it can be faithful to our calling.

PART FOUR

THE MEMBER
OF A MISSION GROUP

VIII.
The Member's
Commitment

Introduction

The making of the member's commitment is the moment for which all the past moments of our lives have prepared us. It is the entering into the explicit and crucial covenant of a people who have pledged to help one another become rooted and grounded in Jesus Christ, Lord of our lives. It is a culmination and fulfillment. Most of all, it is experienced as a joyful and yet frightening beginning of an "immense journey," with a people committed to caring for each other, and to caring for the stranger, the alienated one, the one who has never told his or her story.

Member's Commitment

I come today to join a local expression of the church, which is the body of those on whom the call of God rests to witness to the grace and truth of God.

I recognize that the function of the church is to glorify God in adoration and sacrificial service, and to be God's missionary to the world, bearing witness to God's redeeming grace in Jesus Christ.

I believe as did Peter that Jesus is the Christ, the Son of the Living God.

I unreservedly and with abandon commit my life and destiny to Christ, promising to give him a practical priority in all the affairs of life. I will seek first the kingdom of God and his righteousness.

I commit myself, regardless of the expenditures of time, energy, and money, to becoming an informed, mature Christian.

I believe that God is the total owner of my life and resources. I give God the throne in relation to the material aspect of my life. God is the owner. I am the ower. Because God is a lavish giver I too shall be lavish and cheerful in my regular gifts.

Realizing that Jesus taught and exemplified a life of love, I will seek to be loving in all relations with other individuals, groups, classes, races, and nations, and will seek to be a reconciler, living in a manner which will end all war, personal and public.

I will seek to bring every phase of my life under the lordship of Christ.

When I move from this place I will join some other expression of the Christian church.

Notes

1. Mission group members are those who are the members of The Church of The Saviour. Membership in The Church of The Saviour means membership in one of its mission groups.

2. Members of mission groups have as a minimum discipline the four church disciplines:
- A set time for prayer each day
- Daily reading of Scripture
- Weekly worship—normally with The Church of The Saviour congregation
- Giving proportionately, beginning at a tithe of one's gross income.

3. Authority is given to those in the group who have discovered their gifts on behalf of the mission. Some of these gifts are:

Spiritual Director	Activist
Moderator	Administrator
Shepherd	Ecumenist
Pastor	Teacher

4. In addition to the four church disciplines, the group will practice those disciplines that are agreed on by the members of the group. For example, many of the groups have the practice of keeping a daily journal and of using a weekly report as one means of accountability and support. In addition, each group has those disciplines essential for the accomplishment of its peculiar mission.

5. Fundamental responsibilities of members are the nurturing of intern members, the determining of group policy, and serving on the church council on a rotating basis.

IX.
Spiritual
Journals

Introduction

Most of the small group members keep a journal on some consistent basis. Though the journals are highly individual, and most often private, examples have been included here so that the reader will have an understanding of the kind of material covered. Probably all of our journals have entries that record encounters with darkness and death as well as with excitement and the breaking of new life. A few of the pages were chosen because they reflect no burning bush or mountaintop experience, but rather slow plodding and the writer's effort to deal with his or her own personal demons.

Journal of Mary Clare Powell

10/8. S. last night was distant and cool and not really caring. Felt the most caring from T. and F. and some pleasure in being with H. And P. was nice too, but I missed feeling like the attractive woman I am, wanted to dance but no one asked me. I might have asked someone. They seem to me so business oriented! So straight and sort of tight. I love *Jonathan Livingston Seagull.*

Where am I going? How will I end up? Where is my joy? I tried to convince myself that I still had it, but I don't. It seems as if my needs are monstrous and will never be met, that I will go around starved all my life. My life seems to weigh heavy on me today. Who will deliver me from the power of this fear, depression, anguish?

I am forced nowadays to live under my own heavy condemnation. I was at a higher and therefore to me better, more advanced place in June than now—happier, wholer, more joyful, attractive, more caring and able to give myself, take risks, receive attention and love, to give spontaneously, freely, in love with my life, optimistic. J remember reading Carl Rogers' description of the stages a patient goes through and finding myself at an advanced one. And now I am low and afraid of people again and not attractive and not especially free and certainly not joyful. And it is a vast comedown, another failure. I am back where I was before and the other state has the quality of a dream or fantasy. I've had a single delicious taste of joy at myself, of self-delight and affirmation and now I have fallen from it.

And even though I want to buy all of myself, in one piece, I still have some huge ponderous judging standard that hates and condemns me now for having failed to continue on where I was. Why was I not able to sustain it, keep going? Why am I back into the old patterns—I hated walking from my car with my laundry today on a beautiful Sunday afternoon, sitting in the park grading papers. It's so much like Baltimore before, and teaching before. And the anguish of loneliness and wondering how to fill up next weekend and thinking of people to invite over. And sort of ducking out of the intense relationship (like L.). There is general despair at where my life is now and not being able to see that it will be any different and not being willing to step out and change it.

And as if it weren't bad enough to be having a hard time, I heap on myself loathing and anger and disgust for not making it, for *failing* to keep going upward. I cannot tolerate any failure or weakness, simply can't see or accept that this is also part of who I am. It is a huge burden and I wish to flow out of it, let go of the tremendous expectations. And I can say that but I don't know how to let go of it, cast it out and off and be free of having to despise myself for not being perfect or at least good. Who will deliver me from this?

I called about therapy. That relieved a lot of pressure and made me somewhat calm—that I had admitted I need help and asked for it. And I suppose on my next high I will be as reluctant to let go and as harsh when I fail. If only I could say—"M.C.P., yes, you were there. Really great place you were in. But you are not there now, and, in fact you were unable to keep it, to hold it to you. But that's OK and you can let go of it (and did, when you started teaching—good for you, you let go) and flow into this new time for you. It's a potential time for new growth and truth brings abundant life. So rejoice at where you are. You are not perfect and no one says you must be. Not even your dead father. And your heavenly Father above all loves you and accepts you as is— now. And then. You are complex and things change for you —flow with all changes. Life is not a problem to be solved, worked on, progressed in, but a mystery, sometimes joy, sometimes pain.

You did fail to be perfect, but if you can buy that, there is

great freedom there. *You do not need to be perfect. You are*
OK. Do you hear? You are free from that burden if you can
buy it, you are free already. Just take it.

10/9. Feel somewhat better today—had a good day at school
with the music and guitar players for my classes and giving
N., my 10th grader, the time she requested to get to know my
7th graders. Felt relaxed and gentle and unhassled and open to
kids and going slow enough to hear them and be there for
them. Went out canvassing for McGovern and it was good to
be with K., my partner, and it was good to see some real people. I lose touch in my own small world. Felt open and giving
and above all, soft and gentle with people, and not afraid. I
liked it a lot today. Thanks, my Father, for a good day.

The conversation with A. was troubling.

Me: Teaching full time is a very different thing from playing
at it, volunteering services at times that are convenient. You
seem to be able to avoid the structures and regulations and
bureaucracy and they don't oppress. Like me last year, my free
year, working in the darkroom with a few kids. Those times
are different, really different, from what teaching really is.

Him: Yes, you're right, and I won't give you my moral
lecture on commitment now.

Me: Good, I can't hear it now. All I know is that teaching
is a lot harder and a lot less satisfying to me now.

Him: Well . . . (his face clouds over and he turns to go.
He goes and I feel him saying: "Well, that isn't the point, is
it?"—the satisfaction one gets. Disapproval is sharp. I feel
put down. But I say as he goes out, "That's important to me
now.")

That last is a statement about where I am. I need satisfaction and pleasure in what consumes most of my days; I think
I have some "right" to it. I don't want to lay down my life
for the cause but to own it, pick it up in both hands and give
it away (my life, that is).

A. has given his life to this struggle of public education, risen to an administrative position where there is real power to change the structure, has succeeded to some extent. And therein is meaning and purpose for him, to be engaged in this particular struggle. But I don't think I want or need commitment to that particular struggle for me.

I stood and he disapproved as though there was something disreputable or dirty about seeking satisfaction for oneself. I have just come to the point where I can say I need satisfaction in what I do, where I can feel it is not totally selfish or immoral to look for it (though not it alone) and I get shot down.

I need to think this whole thing out—decide whether it is just my old fear of committing and staying and therefore (to me) dying or whether my feelings now are real things that I should operate on the basis of. All I know today is that, whether because of teaching or what, I have less joy now than last year, that I am surviving minimally, without really enough. Maybe that's enough to know today.

Journal of Ed Schnedl

The following sermon, preached by Ed Schnedl, July 16, 1972, consisted primarily of readings from his Journal.

I came to The Church of The Saviour in 1967 while a student at Virginia Theological Seminary. I came as an observer hoping to glean ideas for my ministry in the Episcopal church in North Carolina upon my return there. I graduated from seminary in 1968. After several turbulent confrontations with my bishop and the examining chaplains, I let my position be known that I intended to change the Episcopal church and I didn't go along with them. They said, "Then don't!" and I didn't. So we parted. They said, "Why don't you stay in architecture? You have a good profession," and I said I thought I would stay in architecture—it was more of the spirit.

So I came to The Church of The Saviour as a rather bitter, beaten, disillusioned man, not knowing what to do with my life. I had had my own architectural practice in North Carolina for twelve years and closed it to enter seminary. I did not feel I wanted to go back to that. So now for four years I have been standing on one foot, not really knowing what to do with my life.

During these four years in The Church of The Saviour, there has been a great deal of healing in myself and my family. Much change has taken place, including my children's growing up and becoming independent. With all these changes I can say that truly this community sustains life as Christ gives it. I feel that Gordon was speaking as Christ when he called me to come forth from the tomb and share with you this morning. I am like Lazarus, when Jesus called on the community of believers who surrounded Lazarus as he emerged from the tomb and said "Loose him; let him go."* It was Jesus who gave him new life; it was the community who took off the wrappings of death. The community helped loose him, and let him go to new life. I feel that my sharing with you is a great privilege and gift from God. It is also a good way for you to take off my wrappings of death.

A year ago last March, Chuck Mottley came here one Sunday and held a healing service. I decided to go to his healing service the following Saturday, and all week I thought about asking for my ulcer to be healed. That Wednesday night the story of the crippled man by the pool came to me. I read it and Jesus was asking me "Do you want to be healed? Do you really want to be rid of that ulcer?" I tried to say Yes, but finally I said No, I didn't want to be healed. I didn't know what I would do without that crutch, my ulcer. I had used it for twenty-four years as my escape hatch. Whenever I wanted to avoid facing the pressure—presto—there was the ole ulcer always dependable. What would I put in its place? I didn't know. But finally I relinquished that ulcer as much as I could, and God healed it after twenty-four years.

This past winter term of the School of Christian Living, I took Betty O'Connor's course in journal writing. There I learned about having a written dialogue with Jesus that just flows as a normal conversation. Many other helpful experiences came from that class for which I am deeply grateful. When I wrote, it came very fast, as if I were taking dictation.

May 7, 1972. Sunday night, late. Had lunch with Bob Gray. I answered his inquiry about my call with an irritated response of being sick and tired of thinking about my call and not wanting to discuss it.

I still do not want to talk about my future. I only want to begin enjoying my life as it is. I want to be carefree. I am sick of wondering about my CALL. I had a thought

* See John 11:38–44.

today of how it might be the same as my ulcer—I prayed so
many years for it to be healed and when I finally realized
I had not really wanted it healed I could face it and offer
it to God and he healed it. But I didn't beat on his chest
for it. I relinquished it to him. I have been pressing so hard
for a good 12–15 years for God to show me what he wants
me to do with my life.

Do I really want him to show me? What will I do then?
What will I fret about? and wring hands about? and I could
lose that good story that is always good for instant demonstration of goodness and of my big sacrifice. How long will
I squeeze blood out of that sacrifice? What pity will I get
when I can no longer blame the Episcopal church for my
plight? What else can I complain about that can keep me
from acting? What will be my excuse then for nonaction?
Do I get myself in a financial bind to keep from acting?

When I can't afford to do something then I can get busy
picking up a little money here and there and it keeps me
busy so I don't have to think about long-range plans. How
much do I use my longing for call? The mystery of God's
call—what is that special thing he has in mind for me?—
with my super talent and super background surely he has
just the right thing for me if I will just wait around for it
and don't go down any blind alleys or get off the track. And
surely it won't have any pain to it or hard work either. It's
going to be easy and all fun and no worries financial or
otherwise. It might be heaven on earth, and after all, it is
my goal to use my gifts and exercise my call and realize my
full potential and fulfillment in my work—isn't that it?
That is salvation—then I won't need God any more, I
won't need the church.

Have I really surrendered? What I have really wanted is
My fulfillment in My work—doing MY THING for God—
if I can just do the right thing I will have arrived. My
sacrifice or offering to God as a full and perfect sacrifice to

him in the sight of men. If it is not known by men will it help anyone?

I see that I have cried out for a clear call when I didn't want to be called. As long as I made motions that looked as if I were really searching, then no one could question or doubt that I really had surrendered. I could have status quo and still appear to be sacrificing my life. I could have my cake and eat it too. All I would have to do is keep trying new things and whenever I got close up on it and it would appear as call then I could back away and just say "Well, it wasn't my call." I better keep searching and keep my time filled up—that was always a good excuse that I could use alternately with the "Sorry, no call."

So the question by Jesus is clear—just like—do you want to be well, healthy?

Jesus: Do you want to be called? Did Peter? Did John the Baptist? [In the Gospel of John:] "What do you want? What are you looking for? If you want to be called, come and see."*

Me: Where do you live, Jesus? I want to know where you're staying—I may want to be called but I don't want you to go off and leave me. Are you for real? Can I count on you to be around? Are you dealing with reality? What kind of security do you offer? Where will I be staying? I may want to be called but I'm not sure. If you are my savior and the savior of the world, where in this world are you staying? How can I follow you if you're not around? If you are the messiah are you going to be around? If you're not staying I don't want to be called. I had the feeling I was abandoned before and during seminary. I really don't know if I trust you. I think I did at one time but maybe it was mere naïveté. I don't know any more. Where are you staying? Are you staying anywhere or are you here today and gone tomorrow? Jesus, I need to know.

* John 1:38, 39.

Jesus: Come and see me and my life. Come and see life and light I give. Come and see my death. Come and see for yourself, not what others have written. Come see me. That is your call. Just see me—be with me, touch me and kiss me and betray me and love me and die with me and rise with me. Come and see me—there is no other call.

* * *

I want to share an experience that happened when writing my journal of July 3, 1972. I had just had a long study period and meditation on the 11th chapter of John. Then I began to write:

Everything points to death and resurrection and that I must die to live. That I must give up everything—ulcer, sacrifice, ministry, call, security, work, home, wife, children, gifts, all things that gave me life as it now is.

At that point I began a dialogue with Jesus in writing:

Jesus, I guess I don't believe you will give life. I believe in some sort of far-removed resurrection. I believe you were resurrected but I don't have enough faith to die. I am loyal like Thomas and I can say "Let's go with him and die with him," but if it's just me all alone when it gets right down to the point of taking up a cross and willingly being tormented by people and spit on and jeered at and ridiculed I can't face it. I need approval, not rejection. I know I seek the approval of men rather than of God—but I am not sure how far you want me to go. I think you're going to have to kill me. . . .

Immediately at this the tears flooded from my eyes as never before. I wept as if for my own death—as if at my own funeral. I felt the very real sensation of signing my own death certificate. I wept as if I were truly dying. After the weeping, which seemed very long though I have no idea how long it was—I would guess fifteen or twenty minutes—then I wrote:

> I cry because I know you'll do it—kill me—and the pain will be terrible. I know I will suffer and be alone—for I know death is solitary. I cry because I will face the blackness and darkness of the satanic. I expose myself in all my weakness. I will be helpless—my cowardice is exposed—I am not brave, I am scared and there is no place to hide from you—you know how I run from pain and I won't have any place to run. Have mercy on me and kill me quickly. I don't know how much I can stand—

Here I broke into more weeping—very intense weeping with tears flowing. Here I was conscious of being exposed, barren and without any protection. I knew there would be no escape—I had to face the pain alone—the prospect was very real—there was no thought about this being fantasy and that I didn't or wasn't now really facing death—it was as if death were here, not that I was actually dying but that I was experiencing now the feelings I would have when dying. I had exposed myself to God's wrath—if he thought I needed to be killed he now had my permission and I knew he would use it. I felt he might literally kill me or he might make me suffer the torments of death without the physical death. So I knew I was in for that suffering and I wept knowing it was soon coming. After the long period of weeping was over I wrote again.

> Lord, I'm like Peter—I can't bear it—the pain. You know who you are and I don't.

It came to me that Jesus knew who he was and his destiny so clearly that he could face the rejection. Peter—and I—

didn't know who we were nor our destiny and therefore could
not stand the thought of torment. It was clear that the
physical pain was not the suffering, because even I felt as if
I could experience the physical death. It was the awful rejection, the torment of humiliation, the being despised that
was the suffering.

I just can't believe all you say is true. I can't give myself
away. I can't even think of others most times. I just think
of myself. I say I believe in you as Lord of my life but I
deny that every day and almost every hour. I am a terrible hypocrite. I lie and I am dishonest. I am envious of
all people who have more than I have in gifts or possessions.
I love to see others fail or suffer if they have more than I do.
I pity those who suffer or fail who have less than I have. I
have so little love for others I am amazed how you tolerate me.

This ended the dialogue. There was a lingering feeling of
being very relaxed and somewhat sad, though not really sad-
ness, but of having come through a stripping away and pulling
off of layers of covering.

From this real suffering of death there has been slow movement. Only in the past week have I begun to feel the promise
of resurrection.

I would like to thank you for taking off the wrappings of
death—loosing me—setting me free—letting me go to new
life. I do not think it would be possible without this community, especially my mission group. Nor would new life for
me be possible without living into the Scripture as we do.
Now I am looking forward with excitement to John 14.

The fact that I feel so good and free to stand here like this
is a sign of new life. I feel so relaxed. I feel great. O Happy
Day!

X.
Letters
of Accountability

Introduction

There are many mechanisms of accountability. A group is not apt to remain disciplined over a long period of time unless the principle of accountability is embraced and a mechanism of accountability adopted.

Perhaps the method most frequently used in our groups is that of the weekly written spiritual report submitted to the group's spiritual director. The director will request the group members to deal with different issues and questions at different times in its life, but each week the members will report faithfulness or laxness at the point of the group's disciplines. Examples of the weekly spiritual report follow. Also included is one person's reflection on a significant period in his life.

Letter of Kathryn Campbell

I have tried to "program" my mind to get down to the business of writing in my journal. So here goes. It will be superficial, but maybe I'll be able to go deeper once I get started.

This past Sunday I went to lunch with two couples and a young man from Philadelphia who had phoned ahead and asked for someone to tell them all about C of S, as they are getting ready to start a "lay parish"—they are Episcopalians.

We had a wonderful time and I talked for about two hours steady. I could have gone on indefinitely because I was in my element. The point I'm getting to is this: After hearing Gordon's sermon about the importance of journal keeping, they wanted to know more about it. Of course I waxed eloquent, then afterward felt like a hypocrite, because look how long I've neglected it. But I'm still sold on the idea and I really believe, if done properly, it's as important as prayer, though not a substitute, of course.

I told them, when they asked me, why it was so beneficial, that it forced you to deal with your hangups and to work on your growing edge.

Another reason I've been so reluctant to send you any more "confessions" is because I seem to still have the same old gripes and can't report any progress. But I'm going to operate on the theory that the reason I still have these hangups is because I haven't gone down deep enough to yank them out by the roots. Maybe this can only be done a little at a time over a long period.

I wake up depressed in the mornings more often than not. It does no good to tell myself this is a physiological sluggishness and all I need is to get up and take a shower and I always feel magnificent, once I do. In fact, morning is my best time, once I get up. Furthermore, I've always got loads of interesting projects lined up. But I always wake up thinking so many pessimistic and hopeless things. The only reason I want to deal with this is I feel that that sort of mood right after deep sleep is an indicator of what's going on in my unconscious. I seldom remember what I've been dreaming about, but it's early in the morning that I try to hold on to whatever it is in order to see where I'm at. That depression takes lots of forms.

I'm sort of a hypochondriac, or a health nut, which is the same thing, I hear. But there's always some little nagging ailment, and I have the feeling that this is an indicator of depression. I say to myself, if I had a dozen kids and a husband to worry over, I'd forget all about my symptoms. If there was always a wolf at the door, I'd quit thinking about these infinitesimal annoyances and get on with more important things. Why don't I lose myself in some great cause?

The thing I'm most discouraged about is that I'm so judgmental. I sit in church on Sunday morning and think mean thoughts about too many people as they come in. This one is silly, that one is dumb, she is extravagant, he is weak, that one is narrow-minded, etc., etc. Why can't I think thoughts of love and blessing and health? Why do I disapprove of a row of hippie types sitting opposite me? Maybe they have a sincere yearning to know Christ. But they're wearing bluejeans and the girl has long hair that covers her eyes, almost! And they aren't singing or joining in the responses. Furthermore, before the service started they were talking to each other and making noise so I couldn't pray.

And why did somebody who came and spoke to me have halitosis? Probably not eating right. And why doesn't that girl stand up straight? She's getting round-shouldered. And why in the world don't people take seats all the way over next to the wall so others don't have to climb over them? Half the time people have to sit out in the hall because they can't even find those hidden seats next to the wall. Furthermore, why don't the people outside SHUT UP when they know we're trying to pray inside?

I've prayed many times to be delivered of all this negativism, but so much still rankles, and new stuff keeps turning up. Woe is me.

It seems to me one of my handicaps is that I'm always thinking in terms of issues rather than being people-oriented. My training and my constant concern for years has been "get the facts straight" and never mind if you step on people's feelings in the process. The irony is that I work in an office full of people who all operate that way, and when they step on my feelings I'm immature and childish (as are they when I do it to them). I suppose the answer to all this is insight, empathy, the compassion of Christ, a larger view of the truth. All of which begins to emerge when you write it down, huh?

Weekly Report of Sonya Dyer

Fasting: I definitely experience a greater awareness of all about me. Also don't miss food or need quantities at other times.

Lk. 19:42, "If only you knew on what your peace depends . . ." The description that follows of being hemmed in, surrounded on all sides by one's enemies, held the personal note of how we let our fears and apprehensions cut us off from those who could bring us life. I also pondered these Scriptures in terms of our missions in the inner city.

Father Delp and Romans: Began working on Romans for my FLOC group. Amazing, the theme of Romans 4, 5, very much like what Delp is saying. Promises, faith, future hope, but also hope in this moment in time and space, joy, endurance, mystery. Great to be in touch with this in two different places at the same time.

Gifts: In using my gifts I must guard against using them as a license to overdo in the area of involvement. Even acts of self-giving coming from the same source can be for good or for evil. My greatest help in holding myself in check is trying to be always aware that I'm not the only one the Lord has commissioned to do his work.

Christmas Advent: Larry had a birthday this week—his 14th. We relived his birthday, the specifics of our household, how the rest of the family fits in, then the different stages of his life and ours, the problems, conflicts, his memories and the like. Led into a discussion of how much of this might also have been true for Jesus growing up, and what it meant to come of age (he shaved for the first time). It was a good time. Our gifting, planning and sharing has been meaningful. I have made something for each of the children, this is my first time at this—this year it seemed right to do this, in other years it would have been forced.

The gift I have been given is a willingness to accept deeply the full idea of mystery. I'm not threatened that my intellect can't grasp everything.

FLOC and City Mission: Came up against the authority of our spiritual director this week in FLOC. He is having us do a verse-by-verse analysis of 10 chapters in Genesis and then answer specific questions. This is not where I am in the exploration of Scripture. I just want to read and try to hear. We had considerable exchange and the matter was resolved for us all. I felt it was a good experience for me and our group in handling our differences creatively.

Outward: I felt moved to write to Rep. Broyhill about the city this week. I have written to him many times before, but this time it was out of the commitment to hope and reconciliation. Compassion is such a missing link. I now feel I can truly pray for him in a new way.

Summary of My Recent Thinking
by Bill Ham

The ways of God with man are very strange. Why should he reserve until the last years of a man's life an insight which, if given at the beginning of that life, would have transformed it? Is this one intimation of immortality? Can it be, as Gordon has often told impatient me, that God's time scale is different from my own, and that an insight given to a man of seventy may be as truly a preparation for a life of joyful service as if that insight had been given to a youth of seventeen?

Recently I have been given such an insight. Through it I have learned three things, all of which I wish I had known when I was younger:

I learned the meaning of repentance.

I learned of the need for suffering, if life is to have meaning.

And I became aware, as never before, of the reality of God and of the nearness and power of Jesus Christ.

Let me go back a bit. Twenty years ago I made my first approach to God. I tried to bargain with him. I said, "If you will spare the life of my beloved wife, I will serve you faithfully the rest of my days."

Of course, it didn't work. Later, after Virginia's death, I came to see how preposterous my attitude had been.

And so, being in touch with The Church of The Saviour, I began my search. Step by step, I gave over one area of my life after another to the fatherly rule of the God of whom I learned through Jesus Christ. But although my life was vastly changed, and great new vistas were opened up before me, there still was something lacking. I believed in God with my mind. I figured things out, and then said, "Yes, it must be so. I'll

160

believe it." But, despite occasional glimpses of another very
different dimension—that of the personal awareness of Jesus
as a Person—the whole thing remained cold, intellectual. God
was, for the most part, remote, mysterious, outside this world
of things, of cause and effect, a cosmic question mark. Did I
really believe that he is what the Bible and the church say
he is? It must be so—but, *is* it? I didn't really feel it in my
bones. My old science-bred scepticism still ruled.

And then, a month ago, came what I can only call a personal revelation, a confrontation with reality. In December
I had gone to my doctor, been examined, and been told that
I was in perfect health. However, there was one small matter
on which it might be well to check. The result of that check:
there is a situation which may be fatal. Operation necessary.
Thus, very suddenly, I was plunged from a consciousness of
perfect health to a confrontation with the possibility of death.
What a drastic change in my outlook!

In this situation, I prayed, and there came to me a perfect
serenity of spirit, an untroubled mind. It seemed surprising
to me that I should feel so untroubled, but there it was—and
I thanked God. Nevertheless, I was perplexed. Was it possible
that my relationship with God, remote and impersonal as it
had been, warranted such a gift? Surely God's ways were
unfathomable. Such was my state of mind right up to the
night before the operation. Grateful, but perplexed.

That evening, as I lay there alone in the bare little room
in a complex of buildings filled with suffering people, I was
suddenly overwhelmed by a devastating thought. What if
this confidence, this sense of security which had accompanied
me up to that point, should leave me? I could not be sure of
its origin. I assumed it came from God—but did it? I certainly
had done nothing to deserve it. It seemed to be a gift, precious
beyond words, but what if it should be withdrawn? Could it
be a self-induced mood which would vanish as suddenly as it
came? What if this life line which had sustained me, this

mysterious serenity that had filled my days, should suddenly not be there?

At that moment I felt that I was on a knife-edge, teetering on the edge of an abyss, wavering like a leaf in the wind. As I looked down, for a flashing moment, I could see myself, bereft of that blessed sense of peace, succumbing to irrational fear and panic. I could see, for a lightning-illumined moment, what it would be like to be alone, lost in the void, deprived of that sense of support. I was tortured by the question: Would that blessed life line, tossed to me so mysteriously from an unknown shore—that wonderful confidence that, come what may, all would be well—would that life line hold?

Then, in that moment of darkness there came to me the words of the 23rd Psalm: "The Lord is my shepherd; I shall not want." And in a flash, the anxiety was gone. The abyss was no longer there, or the anguished questions which rose out of it. I was no longer alone. In that bare little hospital room I was suddenly aware of an enveloping confidence and strength and assurance that seemed to me like the Presence of the Good Shepherd himself. "Yea, though I walk through the valley of the shadow of death, I shall not fear, for thou art with me."* I knew now what those words meant. I knew as never before. And I turned in prayer to the Great Shepherd. His rod and his staff, they strengthened me . . . and the night was full of that peace which passeth understanding. So was the next morning, as I lay waiting outside the door of the operating room, and so were the days that followed. Now, as never before, I could really say: "The Lord giveth and the Lord taketh away. Blessed be the Name of the Lord."‡

From this experience I have learned something new about repentance. Emil Brunner says that, unless one feels profoundly sorrowful over his sin, he is not really repentant. I never felt that way—only a mild regret. But now I was gripped

* Ps. 23:1, KJV.
‡ Job 1:21.

by an indescribable sorrow that earlier in my life I had not
lived in such a way as to be given this wonderful sense of
nearness to God. What a glorious thing it would have been to
have lived a whole life long like that! At the same time, however, that I felt this bitter regret, I was buoyed up by a profound assurance that, late as it was, I had really *turned* away
from the old self-centeredness and was now centered on the
love and the mercy of the Good Shepherd. And I remembered
that the word "repentance" literally means a *turning*—a being
born again—from death to life. At last I was truly repentant.

From this hospital experience, too, I have learned about
suffering. I understand now how suffering, which I, like most
normal people, have always abhorred, can be a great gift, a
source of blessedness and joy. I had never understood how
one could say: "Thank God for suffering!" Now I knew. I
had suffered acutely, even if for a short time. Out of that
suffering had opened a door into a new life. Suffering, which
had seemed something hateful, to be avoided at all costs, had
turned out to be the stepping-stone to a new awareness of
God, through whom, in complete serenity, I could embrace
pain and the possibility of death. For the first time I really
understood what Gordon has said so many times, that suffering can be redemptive, the key to eternal life—and that a
life without suffering is not really life at all, but is life without
meaning.

From this experience, too, I have laid hold again on the
truth, glimpsed in the past, but never really made a cornerstone of my life, that God, the Loving Father, and Jesus
Christ, his Son, together with the Holy Spirit, are a loving
personal Presence—a Savior, Companion, and Friend. For
twenty years I have been reading books and talking to Christians who asserted that this is so. At times I even had a vivid
impression that this might be a reality in my own life. But
always the vision slipped away. The scepticism, the fear of
mere emotionalism, returned, until I wondered sometimes

whether it wouldn't be more honest of me to transfer my allegiance to the remote Old Testament God of Judaism rather than pretend to worship the Christlike, near-at-hand, personal God of the Christians. But recent events have changed all that. That night in the hospital room, and thereafter, I became aware, as never before, of Christ as a Living Presence and Power, immediately accessible—the Good Shepherd, the Light of the World, the Way, the Truth, and the Life—through whom the peace and serenity and love of the Father flowed into my soul. And I am sure now that, for the rest of my life on this earth, and for all of the life to come, I can say, as I have said before in this chapel—only now with a thousand times greater conviction—that I am absolutely convinced that "neither death, nor life, . . . nor things present, nor things to come, . . . nor height, nor depth, nor anything else in all creation, shall be able to separate me from the love of God in Jesus Christ our Lord."*

February 23, 1969

* Rom. 8:38–39, rsv.

PART FIVE

THE MISSION GROUPS OF THE CHURCH OF THE SAVIOUR

XI.
The Mission Groups
of The Church of The Saviour
A Brief Description of Their Outward Journeys

THE ALABASTER JAR

The group was called together around creativity and the conviction that at its heart, the gospel of Christ frees a person to use his gifts. Each member of the group is committed to serious pursuit of an art: painting and drawing, photography and film-making, music, sculpture, poetry. Some members are making a living as artists, some have given up full-time jobs to do their art, still others are at the beginning—exploring their own creativity in one area or several. Members are accountable to each other by adopting artistic disciplines as well as spiritual ones. In their life together, they want encouragement and support—emotional, physical, financial, spiritual, artistic—from each other, and are struggling to evolve the structures that give them this life. As members come into their own as artists, they are able to evoke gifts and creativity in the larger Church of The Saviour community, by dialogue with persons exploring their own creativity and by encouraging sharing of creations in a gallery in the headquarters building. Several members are working at the point of creativity with a group of children. Others are setting up an artists' studio-darkroom in the basement of an inner-city apartment building. The group states, however, that "doing our art—not projects—is our call. But as we engage in this process, we evolve structures by which we give away, for the world's healing, our art and ourselves."

CHILDREN'S EDUCATION

The mission of the Children's Education group is to further, and not hinder, the vital relationship to Jesus Christ of each child in The Church of The Saviour community. They believe that the children are daily asking the questions which pertain to life and death. Members of the mission carefully and prayerfully work on creating the climate and structures for growth that will enable the children to experience their own church community in its totality; to hear Christ's call in their lives; to grow in personal disciplines and to connect prayer and inner life with outward mission. An important group responsibility is the recruitment of class leaders through prayer and personal contacts.

Children above six meet in mission groups that they choose themselves. The mission groups convene around the adult leader's interest. The feeling is that adults communicate most successfully to children in the areas in which they themselves are committed. Like adult groups the children's mission groups have an outward journey as well as an inward journey. One is working in the area of park beautification, and spends some time on Sunday morning working in the parks that are in the neighborhood of the church. The children's old age mission group helps once a week with serving meals to older persons in the adult dinner program. Other groups are working with nutrition, photography, flower arrangements, art, and literacy. The hope is that the small, mission group structure will provide vehicles by which the children can run toward a saving relationship with Jesus Christ.

CLUSTER 70

This group is on mission to let people know they are special, unique and loved, to hold them while they shake and then help them to experience healing and the redeeming community. Members of the group have been trained in counseling techniques and skills, and have made themselves available to others in the community. Recently the group has established a counseling center in the neighborhood of The Potter's House. Counseling will be provided at modest cost to the emotionally and spiritually poor and oppressed who are also economically poor and oppressed.

DUNAMIS

Dunamis is a call to be church to those in positions of political power. The Dunamis groups sense an urgent need to build relationships of love, prayer, and prophetic witness with those who carry decision-making responsibility for our nation. They believe that the power (dunamis) of the Holy Spirit described in the Book of Acts can break into our national life and smash the systems of death and oppression that keep us from being fully human. Dunamis members are committed to daily prayer for one member of Congress, study of the Scripture, an in-depth study of one national issue, and the building of a "pastor prophet" relationship with a member of Congress. Washington Dunamis members are available for the nurture of Dunamis groups emerging in the home districts of the congressmen whom they serve.

FLOC (FOR LOVE OF CHILDREN)

An ecumenical mission started by The Church of The Saviour and neighbor churches to serve abandoned, abused, and neglected children. Starting in 1965 FLOC's initial goal was to replace Junior Village—an oversized 900-bed public institution—with homes or homelike situations for children requiring public care. Junior Village was closed in 1973. FLOC served as a catalyst for the change by persistent advocacy of the plight of neglected children with the local and federal structures of government and by developing foster homes for 100 children. FLOC continues to develop and operate foster homes, relates volunteers to families seeking help with survival problems in order to prevent children from becoming public wards, fights for the interests of neglected children as a class through court action, legislation, and "watchdogging" the public system, and is providing alternatives for children submerged in failure patterns as described below.

FLOC WILDERNESS SCHOOL

A year-round residential therapeutic camping program designed as an alternative to public correctional and other institutions for boys with serious social and behavioral problems. Many children who cannot be reached through verbal counseling can be reached through the outdoor life. In building their own shelter, cutting their own firewood, planning their own activities like backpacking and taking canoe trips, they find outlets for their energies and frustrations. Immediate problems are faced in "problem sessions" anytime during the day and can last from five minutes to five hours. The program revolves around the basic units of two counselors and ten boys who create a mini-community in which they learn to exchange alienation for cooperation and evasion for trust. The average stay is a year to eighteen months. The camp is located an hour and a half from Washington near a national forest. A mission group undergirds and guides the program in conjunction with a ten-person staff.

FLOC LEARNING CENTER

An alternative school for foster and other children whose emotional needs and learning disabilities prevent them from progressing in the public schools. Its aim is to intervene with the child through an individualized program designed to establish a series of small successes. As the child develops learning momentum and is able to manage his behavior in a group setting he is ready to return to the public school and cope successfully. The Learning Center is located in the inner city and has spaces for twenty-four children with a staff of seven. It too like the other FLOC programs is undergirded and guided by a mission group.

GATEWAY

A group called to meet the needs of the many newcomers and visitors to The Church of The Saviour. Members sponsor the Lunch Bunch at one o'clock on Sundays and the Gateway Fellowship Group which meets at the church on Monday evenings at seven o'clock. This fellowship group is open to anyone who wishes to experience Christian community.

JUBILEE HOUSING

Thousands of Washington's poor are living in substandard, unsafe, rat- and roach-infested buildings in deteriorating areas while paying higher rents than the affluent. Members of this mission group are working long hours to change this housing picture in Washington and provide clean, attractive space for persons regardless of their ability to pay. Central to their strategy is the purchase and renovation of decaying and abandoned structures which are in abundance in this and every major city. The project began with the purchase and renovation of several single family dwellings. A committed real estate developer caught the vision of the group and purchased on its behalf two deteriorating apartment houses in the neighborhood of The Potter's House. The Jubilee Housing mission began managing the buildings on November 1, 1973. At present forty-five of the ninety units have been renovated, with a reasonable estimate of 20,000 hours of donated labor.

The human need of the two buildings is staggering. All the classic urban problems accentuated by economic poverty are concentrated there. The usual contacts between management and tenants provide opportunity for knowing and understanding these noble, struggling people. The mission group members are now in the process of establishing a Jubilee Freedom School. As new hope emerges in the tenants, they become part of the team helping to make the apartment buildings work. As progress is experienced by individuals, the group believes calls will be heard to expand this life-giving ministry to other apartment houses and then to other blocks in the city. Better than anyone, the poor know the meaning of discouragement and despair, and the importance of bringing hope to others thus trapped. Members of the group will work with the tenants to give leadership to this movement of freedom and hope for others.

JUBILEE NEIGHBORS

This group is called to create a sense of community in the one block behind The Potter's House in which the two Jubilee apartment houses are located. This one block consisting of five hundred people is diverse enough to provide an exciting dynamic. It is small enough to provide a ministry in depth to every family which wants to participate. Thus far, the group has worked primarily in the Jubilee apartment houses helping in the creation of numerous mini-institutions serving a wide variety of human needs. One member is working in the renovation of a basement room which will be used for a coffee house, another is establishing a "good as new" store which will handle clothes and household items. A teacher in the group is bringing into being an innovative program for children. The doctor in the group worked with a health care program which gave every person in the building the opportunity of a physical examination by qualified doctors and nurses. Mission group members are helping to coordinate the labors of persons from every walk of life—doctors, electricians, legislators and students who feel that they are being given what so many search for—a way to translate their compassion into hope for the city.

LITERACY ACTION MISSION

Two out of three adults in the world are illiterate and one of every ten adult Americans is functionally illiterate. Within the District of Columbia alone there are over *one hundred thousand* functionally illiterate adults and, in addition, there are thousands of youths who are failing to learn to read under our public school system. Those of Literacy Action have committed their lives to meeting this need. They work with individuals, train groups of tutors, and provide coordinators for such groups working in different areas of the city. They seek to reach people in three distinct categories: adults, youth and speakers of other languages. The real miracle occurs when the "helped" becomes "helper." As soon as the nonreader begins to learn and builds confidence, he in turn, receives training and takes on his or her own pupil, while continuing his or her own studies. In little over a year and a half, members of the group have trained close to two hundred tutors. Group members state that while this may seem impressive, in the face of the need it is but a small beginning. They plan to raise continually the issue of literacy and to expand their work in the city, but they have agreed not to solicit funds, but rather to seek the needs of their mission through prayer.

MUSTARD SEED

Members of this group are concerned with the play life of children in the inner city. They had been working in the area of housing when they fell heirs to a toy library that had been set up in Washington by the National Institute of Mental Health. NIMH had run out of funding for its project and was glad to give its large supply of toys to responsible persons who would make them available to children. The toys are now housed in an old restaurant on a main street in the Adams-Morgan area of Washington where preschool children and their mothers go to select toys. If a child returns a small toy three times she or he can borrow better toys.

NEW LIFE

The members of the New Life Mission Group work with the processes of confession and affirmation both in their own lives, and in the group experience of other mission groups. They are available to other groups in the church to help them deal with obstacles to new life. Various exercises and other vehicles are used to facilitate the confession of problems and feelings which block the group in terms of personal relationships within the group, and the actual tasks of mission on the outward journey. They also are available to help groups to call forth and affirm the gifts of individual members for the life of the group and for the work of mission.

POLYCULTURAL INSTITUTE MISSION

This group is the newest of the mission groups. It is working to help bring into existence a low-cost, meaningful, cross-cultural, living, learning experience for a small community of students. The students will be drawn from a number of nations and cultures, and be housed in apartments of the Jubilee

Housing project. The faculty will donate their time and the students will work with the Jubilee Housing mission in the renovation of apartments to help with their rent and food. At this time there is enough commitment and joy in the concept of the institute for the mission members to be reasonably sure that the institute will be off the ground in 1975. One thousand letters were sent to students all over the world to assess their response to the idea and over two hundred responded asking to join in the program. For the initial program only twelve students will be admitted. Mission group members will participate in projects of the institute and support its activities in every way possible. They also want to convey the vision of the Polycultural Institute to other churches and the small polycultural communities that are evolving to study the critical world problems such as food, economy, housing, enrichment, races, nationalism. Members feel that they may be able to work with coordinating the efforts of these communities for the enrichment of all.

THE POTTER'S HOUSE

A rustic, candlelit coffee house in the inner city, open weekdays for lunch and six nights a week until midnight. Through The Potter's House, the mission groups that staff it say to the milling thousands in the nation's capital, "We will serve you, we will be with you in the way in which you naturally gather." The walls of The Potter's House are a gallery for young artists. In one corner of the spacious room is a bookstore carrying selected books to help those who are on a serious inward-outward journey.

Each of the groups that staff The Potter's House has its own emphasis. The Monday night group presents speakers who raise for dialogue the important issues of hunger, war, urban renewal, government and theology. On Tuesday nights, when it is closed, the mission groups may use the coffee house to present special programs. The Wednesday night mission has race relations as its area of concern, and from time to time presents a speaker on this subject. The Thursday night group is seeking to become more practiced in the art of "work and contemplation," and patrons are served in an intentional climate of prayer and meditation. The Friday night group has a special ministry to the Spanish-speaking people who live in the neighborhood. Saturday is an unstructured evening when many out-of-town visitors come. Sunday night is a time for musicians and poets to perform.

On each of the nights the members and intern members seek to live into the servant role toward those who come through the door from busy Columbia Road. They wait on them at table, and are eager to be in conversation when they are invited. The whole atmosphere of The Potter's House is a listening, caring one. Some seek it out because it affords protected corners for quiet meetings with friends. Others come with special problems seeking someone with whom they can talk. In addition to its everyday work of feeding and caring for people, The Potter's House has for its mission the renewal of the whole city, and is a seedbed for new missions, as well as a support for existing missions in the area of housing, education and business.

POTTER'S HOUSE SENIOR COMMUNITIES

A mission concerned with persons who have reached their later years. The group offers an alternative life to senior citizens who are without family or community and who are isolated because of economic reasons. The church purchased a house for this mission's use in the neighborhood of The Potter's House. The group has turned it into a model neighborhood center, adaptable to all economic or social strata. It is a place where seniors have come to know and care about each other, where they have continuing educational opportunities and craft classes and where a nutritious meal is shared each day. Concerts, theatre, picnics, sight-seeing and exercise classes have top priority in group activities. A job referral service, rent supplements and transportation for personal business are presently available on a limited basis, as is personal counseling. The long-term vision is to bring about a complete change in structures and attitudes toward aging that presently interpret retirement as withdrawal from life. The call is upon each group member to share this vision and to deal realistically with his own aging and dying.

RETREAT MISSION

The group is concerned with the life of prayer, meditation, and contemplation. The focus of this mission has been the continuing life of a retreat center at the church farm called Dayspring. The group plans an annual weekend silent retreat for each mission group in the church. There are also open retreats each year to which anyone can come. Leadership is provided by members, the group, or by noted spiritual leaders from around the world. This year one of the members of the retreat group has moved to Dayspring as the resident retreat master, available for group retreats or any who come for personal retreat guidance.

THE SHEPHERD'S GROUPS

These groups are responsible for the three nights of the School of Christian Living. Some members are teachers, some assist teachers, some are administrators. Each member, whatever his or her specific task, seeks to be a shepherd and is involved in enabling those in the school to discover their gifts and respond to the call God has upon his or her life. The school has three eleven-week semesters each year and offers the courses considered basic to an understanding of the Christian faith: Old Testament, New Testament, Christian Doctrine, Christian Growth, and Christian Ethics. In addition, the school offers many elective classes, each of which is concerned with an important aspect of man's multidimensional nature. Each class has as its essential purpose the preparation of members for mission. When a member joins the church she or he is, in effect, ordained to the ministry, and the School of Christian Living is the seminary. The Shepherd's groups are continually seeking new ways to facilitate the goals of training for mission and of providing dynamic structures for healing. An important part of the evening is the informal meal that precedes the classes. This is a time when lives are shared and visions for the future are given. Always the groups are engaged in the designing of new classes, discovering those with the gift of teaching, and exploring training possibilities that exist for potential leaders.

THRESHOLD

The mission of this group is central to that of The Church of The Saviour: worship. Focusing on the Sunday services, the group prepares the bulletins, serves as ushers, coordinates the music, chooses in advance and prays for those who will represent the community in collecting the offering and in distributing communion, and bakes the communion bread. Acting as hosts during the fellowship times which follow the worship services, the group provides information and assistance to newcomers and visitors. Among their other important worship-related activities are the building of fellowship through special events for the community at the Headquarters and at Dayspring, reaching out to newcomers through social gatherings intended to help them become better acquainted, and producing special materials such as litanies.

WELLSPRING

Through this mission The Church of The Saviour shares the life of its community with the church at large. Wellspring provides an in-depth three-year experience through which twenty to thirty participants from all over the country may spend brief periods each year at The Church of The Saviour. Those participating in the program are assigned a spiritual director who maintains a close year-round learning, growing relationship. The mission seeks to share the full dimensions of the inward-outward journeys of individuals and mission groups in The Church of The Saviour. Special attention is given to the inner life of discipline and discovery, the concept of gift-evoking, the strength that comes from outward silence and inward quietness and listening, the enrichment of prayer and the development of personal spiritual disciplines and the realization of personal call. They provide an opportunity to meet with the various mission groups of The Church of The Saviour and to come to know the patterns through which this particular community is learning to aid the rebuilding of people and the rebuilding of a city.

Other books from
THE CHURCH OF THE SAVIOUR
by ELIZABETH O'CONNOR

CALL TO COMMITMENT

"This is nothing less than a disciple's
handbook - a guide on how the individual
and the congregation can be disciples.
The total effect is one of a loving
attitude toward people coupled with a
spirit of inquiry and a humility toward
the Lordship of the Spirit of Christ,
forever turning the intense heat of
encounter into the finest gold of growth
and glory." -- Book Review Service

JOURNEY INWARD, JOURNEY OUTWARD

"The remarkable story of how the Church
of the Saviour is experimenting with
new forms of ministry and worship,
rediscovering the elements of traditional
Christian discipline, freeing its people
for the inward journey of self-discovery
and the outward journey of service."-
- America

OUR MANY SELVES

"A Spiritual workbook for the individual
who wants to come creatively to grips
with life. Material used comes from
the mystics of all ages, from the Gospels,
from the Old Testament, and from the
heart and experience of Elizabeth,
O'Connor. An invitation to maturity and
a challenge to spiritual growth.
Recommended." -- Library Journal

EIGHTH DAY OF CREATION

"In Eighth Day of Creation...Elizabeth
O'Connor tells of her participation in
a process that enables a small group to
uncover each member's unique gift for
the group, God and the world...Also
included are exercises and meditations
...for the discovery of one's gifts...
Church groups serve many purposes.
However, it may be that there is no
more important goal than to uncover,
confirm and share our creative gifts
from God as we, being made in God's
image, do in our 'eighth' day of
creation what God has already done for
us and the world." --The Christian
Century.

SEARCH FOR SILENCE

"In this hurly-burly world, the art of
contemplation, the art of quietness,
seems to be lost yet is longed for by
many. Search for Silence is both a
textbook and a workbook for the serious
seeker...This book offers a unique and
appealing approach to confession,
prayer, contemplation, and the inevitable resultant action...It is a
book to buy, not borrow." --Dimension

THE NEW COMMUNITY

"Elizabeth O'Connor writes with
eloquence and honesty about a very
human and spirit-filled community.
She tells the story of many persons
and of the Church of the Saviour and
of missions that emerge to engage human
need in the city and beyond to build
a community. That it seems to me is
the heart of what the Biblical people
of God is all about. This book will
be exceedingly useful to clergy and
laity in congregations and all who
seek a fresh story about what it is
to be the Church today."- Robert Raines

LETTERS TO SCATTERED PILGRIMS

"What began as personal letters of
encouragement to her fellow "pilgrims"
becomes, in Elizabeth O'Connor's
skilled hands, a broad, perceptive
presentation of contemporary spiritual
themes. They were written during a
transition period in which the Church
of the Saviour was reformed into six
new church communities. Impassioned
and deeply committed, these letters
consider complex and often anguishing
issues, including leadership, authority,
separation, dependence and independence,
and God's call. Especially pertinent is
her discussion of the role of money in
the Christian community. Letters to
Scattered Pilgrims opens new dimensions
of spiritual growth and social concern."
"Sane, Balanced, searching, incisive." -
Douglas V. Steere

ORDER FORM

Name_____

Address_____
                Street

_____
      City   State   Zip

Please send me:

_____copies of Handbook for Mission Groups
    @$3.95
_____copies of Call to Commitment @$4.95
_____copies of Journey Inward, Journey
    Outward @$4.95
_____copies of Our Many Selves @$.495
_____copies of Eighth Day of Creation @$4.95
_____copies of Search for Silence @$4.95
_____copies of The New Community @$4.95
_____copies of Letters to Scattered
    Pilgrims @$6.95

    (Add $1.00 for postage and handling
       for one book, for each additional
       book add 25¢)

Bill me____   Payment enclosed____
       (add appropriate tax)

Please send Order Forms to:

THE POTTER'S HOUSE
1658 COLUMBIA ROAD, N.W.
WASHINGTON, D.C. 20009

ORDER FORM

Name_____

Address_____
                    Street
          _____
          City   State   Zip

Please send me:

_____copies of Handbook for Mission Groups
       @$3.95
_____copies of Call to Commitment @$4.95
_____copies of Journey Inward, Journey
       Outward @$4.95
_____copies of Our Many Selves @$.495
_____copies of Eighth Day of Creation @$4.95
_____copies of Search for Silence @$4.95
_____copies of The New Community @$4.95
_____copies of Letters to Scattered
       Pilgrims @$6.95

     (Add $1.00 for postage and handling
        for one book, for each additional
        book add 25¢)

Bill me____   Payment enclosed___
        (add appropriate tax)

Please send Order Forms to:

THE POTTER'S HOUSE
1658 COLUMBIA ROAD, N.W.
WASHINGTON, D.C. 20009